Tucholsky Wagner Zola Scott Sydow Freud Schlegel
Turgenev Wallace Fonatne Twain Walther von der Vogelweide Fouqué Friedrich II. von Preußen
Weber Freiligrath Frey
Fechner Fichte Weiße Rose von Fallersleben Kant Ernst Frommel
Hölderlin Richthofen
Engels Fielding Eichendorff Tacitus Dumas
Fehrs Faber Flaubert Eliasberg Zweig Ebner Eschenbach
Feuerbach Maximilian I. von Habsburg Fock Eliot Vergil
Ewald London
Goethe Elisabeth von Österreich
Mendelssohn Balzac Shakespeare Dostojewski Ganghofer
Lichtenberg Rathenau Doyle Gjellerup
Trackl Stevenson Hambruch Droste-Hülshoff
Mommsen Tolstoi Lenz Hanrieder
Thoma von Arnim Hägele Hauff Humboldt
Dach Verne Hagen Hauptmann Gautier
Karrillon Reuter Rousseau Baudelaire
Garschin Defoe Hebbel
Damaschke Descartes Hegel Kussmaul Herder
Wolfram von Eschenbach Dickens Schopenhauer Rilke George
Bronner Darwin Melville Grimm Jerome Bebel
Campe Horváth Aristoteles Federer Proust
Bismarck Vigny Barlach Voltaire Herodot
Gengenbach Heine
Storm Casanova Tersteegen Gilm Grillparzer Georgy
Chamberlain Lessing Langbein Gryphius
Brentano Lafontaine
Strachwitz Claudius Schiller Schilling Kralik Iffland Sokrates
Katharina II. von Rußland Bellamy Raabe Gibbon Tschechow
Gerstäcker
Löns Hesse Hoffmann Gogol Wilde Gleim Vulpius
Luther Heym Hofmannsthal Klee Hölty Morgenstern
Roth Heyse Klopstock Kleist Goedicke
Luxemburg Puschkin Homer Mörike Musil
Machiavelli La Roche Horaz
Navarra Aurel Musset Kierkegaard Kraft Kraus
Nestroy Marie de France Lamprecht Kind Kirchhoff Hugo Moltke
Laotse Ipsen Liebknecht
Nietzsche Nansen Ringelnatz
Marx Lassalle Gorki Klett Leibniz
von Ossietzky May vom Stein Lawrence Irving
Petalozzi Knigge
Platon Pückler Michelangelo Kafka
Sachs Poe Liebermann Kock Korolenko
de Sade Praetorius Mistral Zetkin

The publishing house tredition has created the series **TREDITION CLASSICS**. It contains classical literature works from over two thousand years. Most of these titles have been out of print and off the bookstore shelves for decades.

The book series is intended to preserve the cultural legacy and to promote the timeless works of classical literature. As a reader of a **TREDITION CLASSICS** book, the reader supports the mission to save many of the amazing works of world literature from oblivion.

The symbol of **TREDITION CLASSICS** is Johannes Gutenberg (1400 – 1468), the inventor of movable type printing.

With the series, tredition intends to make thousands of international literature classics available in printed format again – worldwide.

All books are available at book retailers worldwide in paperback and in hardcover. For more information please visit: www.tredition.com

tredition was established in 2006 by Sandra Latusseck and Soenke Schulz. Based in Hamburg, Germany, tredition offers publishing solutions to authors and publishing houses, combined with worldwide distribution of printed and digital book content. tredition is uniquely positioned to enable authors and publishing houses to create books on their own terms and without conventional manufacturing risks.

For more information please visit: www.tredition.com

Round Games with Cards A Practical Treatise on All the Most Popular Games, with Their Different Variations, and Hints for Their Practice

W. H. Peel

Imprint

This book is part of the TREDITION CLASSICS series.

Author: W. H. Peel
Cover design: toepferschumann, Berlin (Germany)

Publisher: tredition GmbH, Hamburg (Germany)
ISBN: 978-3-8491-6771-4

www.tredition.com
www.tredition.de

CONTENTS.

———

"NAP," or "NAPOLEON."

The game of Napoleon, or as it is more generally and popularly called "Nap," was introduced into this country from the United States, it is believed, about 1865, although it is recorded that the game had previously been played for high stakes at some of the more notorious gambling clubs.

It is named after the great Napoleon, as the principal player in the game becomes, for the time being, an Ishmaelite, whose "hand" is against every man's, and every man's against his, as was the case with the "Grand Adventurer" in 1804–15 (*see* Variations)—whence we have the terms Wellington, Blücher, etc.

It is an admirable game for three, four, or five persons, and is also available for two and six, though four is the ideal number, and it is played with an ordinary pack of fifty-two cards. (For Nap with thirty-two card pack, *see* page 14). With six persons taking part in the game the dealer stands out of the play, not dealing any cards to himself, though he receives and pays for the tricks like the others, and the same system is sometimes adopted when there are five players; as, if all the players took active part in the game, it would become most difficult to make the tricks, because more cards would be in use.

The popularity of the game is no doubt owing to the short time necessary for playing the hands, and to the fact [4] that it can be terminated at any moment, for no game or deal need exceed two or three minutes, except when a pool or "kitty" is introduced (*see* Variations). In this case provision has to be made for the distribution of the amount of the kitty.

While care in playing is necessary, no great amount of skill is required to render the game diverting as an amusement, while it also affords ample scope for the exercise of speculation and the other elements of excitement.

The main idea of the play, as already stated, is for one of the competitors to stand against the united efforts of the others, who, in turn, use their powers to prevent his securing the object for which he is striving—in this case to win the whole or a certain number of tricks. The number of the tricks to be won is variable, and it depends on the value of the cards in each player's hand to decide what number he will endeavour to secure. The greatest possible achievement is to win the whole of the tricks (which are five in number), and theplayer who succeeds in doing this scores a "Nap," and receives double stakes from each of his companions; if however, after declaring his intention to try for Nap he fails, he only pays a single, *i.e.*, for five tricks; and, as will be shown later on, this condition attaching to a Nap becomes an important feature in deciding on the number of tricks to be played for, when a good hand is secured.

The only safe and perfect Nap is ace, king, queen, knave, and ten of the same suit, but as this combination of cards does not often occur in actual practice, it remains for the player to speculate on his chances with the cards he holds. [5]

It is this speculation of possibilities which forms the principal feature of the game, and it is the ability of a competitor to make an immediate decision on this point that governs his success or failure in its practice. Very much, however, depends on the temperament of the player. A bold, enterprising person will risk much in the hope of winning much, and one player will declare for Nap on the same cards which another would consider only safe for three tricks, and, in like manner, one will declare for three tricks where his neighbour would hesitate to risk two.

Another important matter for consideration is the number of players engaged, and the consequent proportion of cards in use. Each player receives five cards, so that it follows, with three players engaged, that fifteen are in use, and thirty-seven remain in the pack unexposed; whereas if five are playing there are twenty-five cards in use, and only twenty-seven remaining unexposed. The calculation necessary is, therefore, as to the probability of certain superior cards being in the hands of the opponents, or remaining in the un-dealt surplus of the pack.

TACTICS.

As a perfect Nap is of such rarity we must content ourselves with substitutes, and in this respect we may regard the following combinations as good ordinary hands on which to declare for the full number of tricks: a flush of fairly high cards, *i.e.*, the five all of one suit; four of one suit (headed with ace or king), and one high card of another suit; or three high cards of one suit, with two high cards of a second suit. It is dangerous to risk a Nap on a hand of three suits, unless it consists of three high cards of one suit with two other aces; then it is often possible to [6] win the five tricks, by first exhausting the trumps, and then playing the aces, which must win; but if one of the opponents starts with four trumps, no matter how small, success is, of course, impossible.

If a player does not consider his cards good enough to permit of his declaring for Nap—and it is fair to suppose that not once in a hundred they will be absolutely safe—he has to decide what they are worth, and declare accordingly. It is not often that four tricks are called, because a hand good enough for four is usually regarded as sufficiently good for Nap, on account of the additional stakes received by the player who succeeds in making the whole of the tricks, which amount to a difference of six points from each competitor, as for four tricks he receives four, while for Nap he receives ten, paying only five, however, if he loses.

On the same principle as already shown in regard to a "perfect" Nap, it will be understood that ace, king, queen, is the only certain combination with which to secure three tricks, but these cards, again, are seldom met with in a hand, and speculation is once more the principal matter for consideration. Ace, knave, and ten of a suit is generally good for three tricks, as the only possibility against such a combination is that one of the other players holds king or queen of the same suit, with a smaller trump to throw away when the ace is led. Three tricks are, however, often called on much lower cards than ace, knave, ten, especially when the other cards in the hand are of one suit, or are sufficiently high to admit of the possibility of one of them securing a trick. The same line of reasoning holds good in regard to a declaration of two tricks, the only certainty in that case being ace and king.

It must not be considered, after these comments on the game, that there is any great difficulty to surmount in acquiring [7] a knowledge of Napoleon. As we said at the commencement of our remarks no great skill is essential, but considerable care is necessary to secure anything like success at the game, the chief factor in which is so-called luck. It is impossible to make tricks, or even declare an intention to try for them, unless one receives a certain number of high cards. One may even go further, and say that luck goes far beyond the actual cards dealt to each player, for the best of hands often fail, and poor cards frequently achieve success; whilst it happens, in numerous cases, that the playing of the cards demonstrates that really weak hands would have secured success if the holder had had the pluck, or impudence, we may term it, to declare more than the value of the cards seemed to justify. On the other hand it is often astonishing to find the number of high cards of a given suit included among the fifteen, twenty, or twenty-five in the hands of the players engaged in the game.

Taking all matters into consideration, it must be regarded as virtually impossible to give any precise rules for deciding the number of tricks to declare, and it is equally difficult to lay down any definite plan for playing the cards to the tricks. We can only generalize for the information of our readers, who must decide for themselves whether they will play an adventurous game, with its greater risks, and greater possibilities of success; or whether they will adopt a quieter and less speculative course, standing to win or lose less on their own declarations.

It must always be borne in mind, however, that whichever course is pursued it is only his own actions that can be governed by each player. One may adopt a quiet, safe game, and risk little, while some or all of the opponents may adopt the opposite extreme, and force all the competitors, [8] in a manner of speaking, to share in their risky speculations. If the bold player wins, and we think the chances are in his favour, the quieter ones, no matter how safe their own declarations may be, must necessarily lose, and *vice versâ* so that we have, not only the numberless possible combinations of the cards to consider, but also the temperament and position of those engaged in each game.

Care should be taken to remember, as far as possible, the cards thrown away by the other players, when they cannot follow suit to any particular lead, and it will be found in practice that much information can be derived as to the character of the remaining cards from a careful study of the hands during the progress of the play, and this knowledge is particularly valuable when a player is left with two cards of equal, or nearly equal value, and his chance of success depends upon his winning a trick with one of them.

We shall now proceed to consider the various parts of the game, and the variations that have been introduced into the method of playing it.

STAKES.

The stakes may consist of any amount previously arranged, and whatever is decided upon, whether it be counters or money, is recognised as the limit per trick, only changed when a player having declared for Nap, succeeds in making it, in which case each player pays double, or as though he had lost ten tricks. In other cases the players win or lose one stake for each trick that the senior hand has declared for. Say, for example, he declared to win three tricks, and succeeded, then each of the other players would pay him three times the amount of the stake; if the senior hand did not succeed, he would have to pay a similar amount to each of the others. [9]

DEALING.

The deal is decided by the cards being turned face upwards before each player, until the first knave is exposed. The player to whom the knave falls then becomes the first dealer. It is better to play with two separate packs of cards, as considerable time is saved in collecting and shuffling, which operations are to be performed by the player on the next dealer's left hand side. When shuffled the cards are to be placed on the right hand side of the dealer, where they are to be left until the player on his right cuts them. The dealer distributes five cards to each player, going from left to might, and dealing the cards one at a time.

As the deal is a disadvantage, inasmuch as the dealer has the last call, there is no penalty attaching to a misdeal, unless the game is being played with the addition of a pool or kitty (*see* page 11), in which case the player making a misdeal pays a penalty to the pool equal to the stake of one trick. In the event of a misdeal, or accidental exposure of a card, the whole pack must be collected, shuffled and re-cut, as before, after which the cards are to be re-dealt by the same player who made the mistake. The players must not interfere with the cards during the deal, under a similar penalty, nor touch the remainder of the pack when once it has left the dealer's hands.

CALLING.

The deal having been completed the players are entitled to look at their cards, and then declare, in turn, whether they will "stand" or "pass," the player on the dealer's left having the first call. If he decide to stand he declares the number of tricks he will stand for, while if he elects to pass [10] he simply states his intention of so doing, but it is understood that the first caller must stand for one trick, should all the others decide to pass, except in the case where the Double Header is agreed to (*see* page 13). The next player then announces his intention. If he cannot stand for more tricks than have already been called he must pass, and the same holds good all round, until the dealer is reached. No player may make a second declaration, or alter one once made.

PLAYING THE HANDS.

The player who has called the highest number of tricks now becomes senior hand, and his object is to make the tricks he has declared, in opposition to the united efforts of the other players, who combine—without consultation or arrangement of any kind—to defeat his purpose. The senior hand may make trumps of any suit he chooses, and this he signifies by leading one of the suit he selects. It will thus be seen that the first card played in each deal decides the trumps for that deal.

The player on the left of the leader then follows. If he has a card of the suit led he must play it, but if not he may throw off any card he chooses. If he has more than one card of the suit he can play either, as he is not forced to head the trick even if he has a card higher than that led but in practice it is seldom desirable to pass a trick in the first round, when headed by the senior hand, except under exceptional circumstances, such for instance as holding ace and a small one, with knave or a lower card led.

Provided no player has headed the trick, *i.e.*, played a higher card of the same suit as the one led, the trick is scored by the senior hand, and he leads for the second [11] round. If, however, one of the players has taken the trick, then the lead passes to the winner of that trick, and the same occurs after the second, third and fourth tricks.

In the second and subsequent rounds the leader may play whatever card he chooses, just as in the first, the trumps remaining unaltered. A player having one of the suit led in either round must play it, but if he has none of the suit he may either discard one of the others, or head the trick by playing a trump. This continues throughout the five rounds, unless the senior hand shall have previously won the number of tricks he declared, or shall have lost such a number as to render his success impossible, in either of which cases the cards are collected for the next deal.

VARIATIONS.

There are several innovations and different methods of play which may be introduced into the game of Napoleon, but any divergence from the plain game should be carefully settled by the company *before the play is commenced*. Failing a proper understanding on this point, the rules applicable to the simple game must be adhered to.

POOL OR KITTY.

When a pool is agreed to, payment is made by each dealer according to the value of the stake of the game, but it is more convenient for all of the players to pay in when it is the original dealer's turn to play. The Kitty thus formed becomes the property of the caller who makes Nap, and he takes it in addition to the double stakes he [12] receives from each player, as already mentioned. When it is found desirable to conclude the game before a Nap has been secured, the amount of the kitty is to be equally divided between the players, or it may be drawn for, in which case a card is distributed to each player by the regular dealer, who has the cards properly shuffled and cut for the purpose, when the holder of the lowest card (ace here reckoning as highest) takes the pool.

MISERY OR MISÉRE.

This is the most common variation, and is the antithesis of Napoleon, inasmuch as the caller must not make a single trick. The caller leads off in the ordinary way—the suit led being trumps, as usual, unless it is agreed, as is sometimes done, that there shall be no trumps in this variation. The caller of misére must always follow suit, if he can, but is not obliged to trump if he has none of the suit led. He must, however, play the cards so as to avoid taking a trick. Should he be compelled to win one of the tricks, or should his original lead remain unheaded by any of the other players, then he fails in his declaration, and has to pay, but if he avoids making a trick, the other players have to pay him. The usual stake for "misery," either for winner or loser, is three; but any player declaring he can make three tricks takes precedence, and plays accordingly.

BUYING CARDS.

After the cards have been distributed, *but before any declaration has been made*, the dealer asks each player in turn, beginning with the player on his left, whether he wishes to buy a card or cards. The player wishing to purchase must first throw away the cards he desires to eject, [13] face downwards, and must place in the pool the value of one trick for each card he desires to receive from the dealer. The card or cards must be taken from the top of the pack, and handed unexposed to the player.

SPARE HAND.

An extra hand is dealt, which each player in turn has the option of adding to his own hand, selecting from the ten cards thus held five with which to play, but he must then stand for Nap, and, if there is a pool or kitty, he must put therein the value of two tricks if he fails to score, in addition to paying each of the players the ordinary stake on losing five tricks.

DOUBLE HEADER.

If each player "passes," then the stakes for the next deal are doubled, and remain so until the person declaring has won. In cases where this variation is decided upon, it is usual to agree that the lowest call be "three," so that the double header occurs at frequent intervals.

WELLINGTON.

If a player calls Napoleon, and another player on his left considers he can also make five tricks, he may call "Wellington," in which case the stakes are doubled, the caller winning 20 or losing 10. As this rule, however, is regarded with disfavour by some, in consequence of its raising the limit of a loss on any particular hand from 10 to 20, it is sometimes played differently. The player who calls Wellington does not receive more than he would have done for Napoleon, but pays double, *i.e.*, 10. [14]

BLÜCHER.

This is called in the same manner, that is to say over the player calling Wellington, and then the stakes are trebled, the caller winning 30 or losing 15.

In the modification of this variety, as referred to in connection with Wellington, the caller would still only receive 10 for winning, but would pay 15 to each player if he lost. This may appear a severe penalty, but it must be remembered that both Wellington and Blücher are declarations outside the ordinary limit of the game, and it is not possible for the first caller to claim them, even though he may have the first five cards of a suit, and therefore be certain of winning everything. He calls Napoleon as the limit allowed by the game, and it is therefore unfair that he should lose the advantages of his good hand.

Another variety of this game is to allow the caller of Napoleon the opportunity of altering his call to Wellington or Blücher if challenged by any of the others to do so. If he thinks he can scare he stands for the higher call; if not, then the player who challenges him does so.

The settlement of these extended calls should be particularly agreed upon before commencing play, or disagreement is all but inevitable, as the player who insists on the forced increase of the limit is certainly in the wrong, unless arrangement has previously been made.

THIRTY-TWO CARD PACKS.

If Piquet or Bézique cards are used, *i.e.*, packs with the 2, 3, 4, 5 and 6 of each suit omitted — leaving but 32 cards in the set — the ordinary rules are observed. When playing with this smaller pack the hands will *apparently* be of far [15] greater value than usual. This arises from the fact that all the lower cards of each suit are omitted, and after a few deals it will be found very difficult to make even a small number of tricks with hands which, if a full pack of cards was in use, would be exceptionally good. There being but thirty-two cards to deal with, the number of players must not exceed three, or perhaps four.

SIX- OR SEVEN-CARD NAP.

In this variation six or seven cards are dealt to each player, who, before making his call, has to throw away (face downwards and unexposed) one or two, as the case may be, of his cards, so as to leave the number in his hand five, when the game is played on the regular lines.

NINE-CARD NAP.

This may be described as the last innovation in the game. It is conducted on exactly similar lines to the five card method, except that nine cards are held by each player, none being discarded as in the last mentioned variation, but it has not yet become popular, and in view of the fact that even with only three players more than half the pack is in use, its scope is far more limited than any other variety. In this variation the person calling Nap would have to make all nine tricks, a most difficult and very unfrequent occurrence. It will be found to be a pleasing variety for two players who are of about equal skill at the ordinary game, its possibilities being so different from that method, but we doubt its ever being made as popular as the five card game. [16]

LOO.

———

Loo (or, as formerly it was sometimes called, Lue) is a very lively and popular round game, justly described as one of the best and yet one of the simplest known. Indeed, until the introduction of "Nap," it was the most fashionable of its class in this country. The date of its origin is not on record, but that some amount of antiquity can be claimed for it may be inferred from the fact that a description of the game appears in works published at the beginning of the present century, when the method of playing it was virtually the same as is recognised at the present day, except that then the five-card variation was the most popular, whereas now the three-card game is in vogue.

Loo is usually played with an ordinary pack of fifty-two cards, but in some variations the thirty-two card pack is used. The number of players who can take part in it is practically unlimited within the range of the pack played with. A writer of thirty years since justly remarks that the game is good for any number up to a dozen, although the best game is played with five, or not more than seven persons. Five players are sometimes regarded as the limit, and if more than that number desire to take part, relief is sought by the dealer standing out of the play, neither paying nor receiving on the tricks of that hand. This arrangement, however, is one that can be decided at the option of the company playing. [17]

As is the case with Nap, a very short time is necessary for completing the hands in the game, and a finish may be made at any moment, either by an equal division of the amount in the pool among the players, or by releasing those who failed to win a trick in the previous deal from the penalty which usually attaches to such a result, and which is known as a "loo." In this case all "stand" on the last round, and there is no "miss." It is usual, however, to play on until what is known as a "single" occurs, _i.e._, when each of the players who declared to stand has secured a trick, and, as a consequence, no one has been looed. If, however, a finish is desired before a single occurs, it is best to arrange it so as to fall immediately before the original dealer's turn to deal comes round again, as, in that case, all the players will have paid for an equal number of deals.

A player may withdraw from the game at any time when it is his turn to deal. In that case he pays for his deal (as explained later on), and also for his loo, if he was looed the previous hand, but he does not deal any cards to himself, or take any part in the play of that round.

DESCRIPTION.

Three-card Loo being the most popular at the present day, we shall devote ourselves more particularly to that game, leaving the five-card variety to be considered later on, under the heading of Variations. The object of each player is to win one, two, or all of the three tricks into which each deal is divided, and in doing so he is opposed by all the other players who have elected to stand, and who, in turn, try to secure the tricks for themselves.

The stakes are first decided on—usually three counters [18] or coins for the deal, and six for a loo. It is desirable that the amount in the pool should be divisible by three, so as to allow of its equal apportionment among the winners of the three tricks. The first dealer is then chosen, and he, having paid to the pool the agreed amount for his deal, proceeds to distribute the cards for what is termed a single, a term denoting that merely the dealer's stake is to be played for.

The pack having been duly shuffled and cut, the dealer turns the top card face upwards in the middle of the table, and then distributes one card, similarly exposed, to each player. If either of the players receives a higher card of the same suit as the one turned up, he wins the amount in the pool. If two or more receive superior cards, the higher takes the stake. The others are looed, each having to contribute the agreed amount of a loo to the pool, for the next deal. It is usually agreed that the penalty for a loo on the single shall be half the amount of the ordinary loo, or the same amount as for a deal. If neither player receives a higher card of the same suit as that turned up all are looed, and the amount in the pool remains, being included in the stakes for the next deal. The amount of the loos having been placed in the pool, as also the sum agreed upon to be contributed by the next dealer, the cards are re-gathered, shuffled, and cut, and the second deal is proceeded with. Three cards are distributed to each player, and a spare hand, or miss, as it is generally called,[1] is left in the middle of the table.

[1] The spare hand is not always called the "miss." Some players designate it the "cat"; the term possibly originating from its uncertainty; hence the expression, often used in connection with the spare hand—"Let us hope she will not scratch us."

The top [19] card of the undealt portion of the pack is next turned up, to decide which of the suits shall be trump, and then each of the players—commencing with the one on the left hand side of the dealer—in turn looks at his cards, and decides whether he will stand, whether he will take the miss, or whether he will throw up his cards for that deal, unless the rule for "Club Law" shall have been previously decided upon, when all the players have to stand, and the miss is withdrawn—see page 26. If he decides to stand, the player retains the three cards originally dealt him, and says, "I play"; if he elects to throw up his cards, he places them, unexposed, on the top of the undealt portion of the pack, and takes no share in the remainder of that hand, neither paying nor receiving in connection with the play; while if he determines to take the miss, his original cards are added to the undealt portion of the pack, as before, and he takes up the spare hand. In this latter case he is compelled to stand, that is, it is not optional with him to throw up the miss, when once he has elected to take it.

The player on the dealer's left having determined which course he will pursue, the one on his left has to decide, and so on, until the dealer is reached; he may, in like manner, stand, throw up, or take miss, provided the spare hand has not already been appropriated. If none of the players take the miss it is added to the pack, but in that case it must not be exposed, or looked at by any of the players.

Should it happen that each of the players in front of the dealer has thrown up his own cards, and neither has taken the miss, then the dealer is entitled to the amount in the pool, no matter what his cards are. Should it happen that only one player has declared to stand on his own hand, [20] then the dealer, if he cannot stand on his own cards, may take the miss. If he does not care to do either he must play the miss for the benefit of the pool, against the single player who declared to play on his own cards, and anything he may then win with the miss is left in the pool for the next deal. Should it happen that all the players in front of the dealer have thrown up their cards, and one has taken the miss, then the dealer may stand, or not, as he chooses; but if he also throws up his cards, then the holder of miss, being the only standing hand, takes the whole amount of the pool. These contingencies are seldom, if ever, met with in actual play, but being possible it is necessary to fix laws to govern them.

The players who have decided to stand, either on their own cards, or on the miss, then proceed to play the tricks, the one nearest the dealer's left having to lead. It is, however, sometimes agreed that the holder of miss for the time being shall lead, but this is hardly a desirable departure from the more regular course of leaving the lead to the elder hand, and we cannot recommend its adoption. If the leader holds the ace of trumps he must lead it, and similarly, if the ace is turned up, and he holds the king, he must start off with that card. If he has two or three trumps (of any denomination) he must lead the highest. "Two or more trumps, lead *one*," is the rule of some players, but unless this matter is specially decided upon before the commencement of play the rule to lead the *highest* of two or three must govern the point. In all other cases the leader may start off with whichever card he chooses.

The play proceeds from left to right, and each player, in turn, has to follow suit if he can; as it is his desire to secure the trick for himself he will play as high as possible [21] if he has the power to head the trick. If he cannot follow suit he must play a trump if he has one, provided his trump is higher than any previously played to the trick, but it is not compulsory to trump a suit when it is not possible to head the trick by doing so. Failing the ability to head the trick, he may discard as he chooses. It is compulsory, however, for each player, in turn, to head the trick if he is able to do so, and herein lies one of the greatest differences between Loo and Nap, for in the latter game, as we have shown, it is optional with a player whether he will head the trick, or pass it. The trick is won by the player who plays the highest of the suit led, or, if trumped, the highest trump. As winner, he has the privilege of leading for the next trick, which is conducted on similar lines to the first. This applies also to the third trick, the only stipulations being that if the player who won the first trick has a trump he must lead it, and if he be left with two trumps he must play the higher of the two as the lead for the second trick. The three tricks having been disposed of the amount in the pool is divided equitably among the winners, while those who stood—-either on their own hand or on miss,—and did not succeed in winning a trick are looed. If all who stood succeeded in making one or more tricks, so that neither of the players was looed, it becomes a single again, and the cards are dealt as already described for that round (see p. 18).

A player infringing any of the rules, or playing in an irregular manner, is looed, and the amount of his winnings, if any, is left in the pool. The hands must, however, be replayed in proper order, and if then the tricks are secured by different players, that must be considered the result of the hand, and the losers by the proper play are looed, even though by the first and erroneous method they secured one [22] or more of the tricks. Briefly, no player can he looed, or secure any part of the pool through the irregularity of either of the other players. In any case the player who transgressed the law does not win anything. If his cards secure one or all of the tricks the amount of his winnings is left in the pool for the next deal, and he is looed. This does not apply to penalties for looking at the hands, or declaring out of turn, or making a misdeal. In those cases the offending player pays the penalty into the pool for the current deal, and stands an equal chance with the others in fighting for the tricks. The cards as played are left in front of the players, not being turned or otherwise interfered with until the completion of the three tricks, when, as already described, they are gathered up for the next round.

We will now proceed to consider the various points of the game not touched upon in the description already given.

STAKES.

For the reason already mentioned the stakes should be so arranged that the amount in the pool can always be divided by three.

Thus, supposing that three counters, or coins, are fixed as the amount for the deal, and six for a loo, there cannot possibly be any surplus after the division among the winners of the three tricks, no matter how many may have paid in. If, however, the pool consists of such an amount as to render equal division impossible, the division is made as nearly equal as can be, and the winners of the first and second tricks have the preference.

It is not necessary that the loo should be twice the amount of the deal, indeed any sum may be fixed for either the one or the other, and it is not unusual when the [23] deal is settled at 1½d. for the loo to be 6d., or when the one is 6d. for the other to be 2s. 6d., and so on. Another method is to make the stake for a loo unlimited, and yet another to make it somewhat of a combination, unlimited up to a certain amount (*see* Variations), but the more general course is to have a definite price fixed (*a*) for the deal, (*b*) for an ordinary loo, and (*c*) for a single loo, which latter is generally half the amount of the full loo.

Before commencing play in the game, it is desirable to settle whether Club Law (*see* Variations) is to be enforced, and whether any alteration is to be made in the law compelling the holder of two or more trumps to lead the *highest* on the original lead. The modification of this rule is "two or more trumps lead *one*."

DEALING.

The deal is settled in the same way as already described in connection with Nap, and the cards having been shuffled and cut, the single is dealt, as described on page 18. In other rounds the dealer must distribute the cards to the players one card at a time, in regular order from left to right, and must deal to the spare hand, or miss immediately after dealing his own card each time. With some players deviation is permitted, the dealer being allowed to distribute the cards in any order he likes, and either singly or three at a time; or the miss is left until last, when the three cards for the spare hand are dealt at once. These departures are not desirable, and we strongly recommend the enforcement of the rule compelling the regular distribution of cards, as herein set out.

In the event of a misdeal, an irregular distribution of the cards, or the exposure of a card during the dealing, the dealer is looed — the amount of the loo in this, and most [24] other cases of penalty prior to the commencement of the playing of the cards being the same as settled for a single loo — and he immediately places the amount in the pool. The whole pack is collected, re-shuffled, and dealt again by the same player, and the game proceeds.

Any player interfering with the cards during the deal is looed, but the cards are not re-dealt, unless they have been mixed, or a card has been exposed.

DECLARING.

The cards having been dealt, and the trump card turned up, the player on the left of the dealer has the right to look at his cards, and declares his intention to stand, throw up, or take miss. He having decided, the player on his left does the same, and so on all round. Any player looking at his cards before it is his turn to do so, or declaring out of turn, or looking at the miss without taking it, or looking at either of the thrown up cards, or at any part of the undealt portion of the pack, is looed a single, and pays the penalty into the pool at once, but he is not debarred by any of these irregularities — - except when he looks at either of the opponent's hands — from taking part in the play of that deal. If he looks at the cards of any other player he is looed the full loo, and must throw up his own cards, unexposed, unless he has already declared to stand, or has taken the miss, in which case he has to play to the tricks, having first paid his loo into the pool; in the event of his cards securing either of the tricks the amount won is left in the pool for the next deal.

No player may make a second declaration, or alter one once made, and a player who decides to stand, or who takes the miss, must play his cards with the others interested in [25] the stakes; he not being permitted to stand out, lest his doing so should affect the others' play.

The players having decided whether they will stand or not, the leader plays his card. If he holds ace, or with ace turned up holds king, and fails to lead it, he is looed; similarly, with two or more trumps if he fails to lead the highest he is looed. Any player neglecting to follow the suit led, when he is able to do so; or omitting to trump a suit, when by so doing he can head the trick, is likewise looed; as also is any one playing out of turn, or exposing or mentioning the value of his own, or opponent's unplayed cards, or of either of those in the miss, or among the undealt portion of the pack.

If the winner of the first trick remains with a trump, and fails to lead it; or having two trumps left fails to lead the highest, he is looed.

In all these cases the penalty is the amount of a full loo, and it is added to the pool for the *next* deal. The cards must he replayed in proper order, and if the player who transgressed wins either of the tricks his winnings must be left in the pool for the next deal.

VARIATIONS.

As mentioned in the case of Nap, any divergence from the plain game must be carefully settled by the company before play is commenced, and failing any special agreement it is understood that the rules of the simple game are to be adhered to. [26]

CLUB LAW.

This is the most common variation, and its object is to force a number of loos, especially when a large number of players are engaged in the game. When it is adopted, all the players have to stand on their own cards, whenever the card turned up for trump proves to be a club. In that case the miss is withdrawn, and is added to the undealt portion of the pack without being exposed.

UNLIMITED LOO.

In this variation the penalty to be paid for a loo varies with the amount in the pool, and becomes the same as the total stakes of the previous deal. By the adoption of this variation a considerable sum may be lost in a very few minutes, and, in consequence, it is not often played outside the regular gambling clubs. Of course the amount goes on increasing by rapid strides until a single occurs, when a fresh start is made with only the stake of the dealer to fight for. At unlimited loo the amount payable for the deal remains unaltered, no matter how much was in the pool the previous round.

MIXED LOO.

This is played on the same lines as the unlimited variation, except that a limit is fixed, beyond which the loo does not go. For instance, suppose the original stakes to be 3*d*. for a deal, and 6*d*. for a loo —- limited to 2*s*. 6*d*., a player would be looed the amount in the pool, up to the limit, but if the amount exceeded the 2*s*. 6*d*., he would not be called upon for a larger sum. [27]

FIVE-CARD LOO.

This is the old-fashioned game, and we may go back to old books for a description of it. It is said to be a much more amusing game than three-card loo for a company not inclined to play for high stakes, but is not suitable for more than six players, even if five should not be regarded as the limit. Each of those engaged in the game has five cards dealt him, either first three, and then two, or one at a time, the latter method being by far the best, and the following card is turned up for trump. There is no miss, but each player has the liberty of changing, for others from the pack, all or any of the five cards dealt him, or of throwing up the hand altogether. If he decides to change any of his cards, the player, whose turn it is to declare, places the cards he wishes exchanged, face downwards, on the table, and the dealer gives him a like number from the top of the pack. No second exchange is allowable, nor can a card once put out be taken back into the hand; neither may a player who makes an exchange afterwards throw up his cards; he must play them out. The knave of clubs generally, or sometimes the knave of the trump suit, as agreed upon, is the highest card, and is styled *Pam;* the ace of trumps is next in value, and the rest in succession, as in the three card variation, where the cards rank in the ordinary way: ace, king, queen, knave, ten, nine, *etc.,* down to the two. Those who play their cards, either with or without changing, and do not gain a trick, are looed. When a flush occurs, that is, five cards of the same suit, or four cards of a suit with Pam, the holder of the flush — who does not declare it until all the players have settled whether they will stand or not — besides taking the amount in the pool, [28] receives from each of the players, whether they stood or not, the amount of a loo, and the next deal becomes a single, there being no payments to the pool, beyond the dealer's fee. A flush in trumps is superior to a flush in any other suit, but if there is more than one flush — neither of which is of the trump suit — then the flush which includes Pam wins, or if neither contains that card then the elder hand, that is, the player nearest the dealer's left hand, scores the flush, and the holder of the other flush takes nothing; he, however, is exempt from the loo, which is payable by the other players. When the ace of trumps is led it is usual for the player of it to say, "Pam, be civil," in which case the holder of Pam must pass the trick, if he can do so without revoking; but if he has no trump he may win the trick with Pam.

IRISH LOO.

This is virtually the same as the five-card variety, except that three cards only are dealt to each player, and Pam is unknown.

As described in connection with Nap, Piquet or Bézique cards may be used for Loo, but in that case the number of players must, of necessity, be more limited, only 32 cards being available. In all other respects the rules applicable to the full packs apply.

——————— [29]

HINTS TO PLAYERS.

I.—Declaring.

In deciding whether to stand on one's own cards, or whether to take the miss, the amount in the pool is a matter for special consideration. With a heavy stake to fight for, a player will run greater risks than when a small amount is available. Therefore, the first question to decide should be the amount per trick in the pool, as compared with the amount to be paid if one is looed.

It is unwise to stand on any hand that does not contain a trump; but if the cards are very high ones, and the amount in the pool warrants it, the risk may be taken.

With very few exceptions a player should stand on two trumps, however small, but the first player should have a tolerably high card, in addition to two small trumps, other wise the hand is a risky one.

An honour in trumps and high cards in other suits are generally safe, especially for the player who has to lead; indeed, the first player may stand on almost any single trump, if his other cards are high ones of different suits—queens at least.

King of trumps with small cards in other suits is generally safe, although cautious players throw up such a hand. Very much depends on the amount in the pool, although we should not reject such cards under any conditions.

Queen or knave of trumps with small cards of other suits are matters which must be left to individual opinion—based on the number

of players and the stake to be played for. They are undoubtedly
risky hands, but if one only stands on certainties half the amusement and all the excitement vanishes.

After a few rounds have been played, a fair opinion can [30] be
formed as to what cards are likely to make a trick, and if the sum in
the pool is considerable, risky cards may be kept, or the miss taken
at an early stage, although it must not be overlooked that the other
players will likewise stand on risky hands, and, as a consequence,
there will be more competition, with fewer chances of securing a
trick.

The first hand should seldom take the miss, nor should either of
the other players if each of those in front of him has decided to
stand on his own cards, as it may be assumed that in such cases
there is strength. With five playing, two of whom have thrown up,
miss may be taken, but with three players standing on their own
cards, miss should not be attempted.

II. — Playing.

The laws of the game define what shall be led with two or three
trumps, or with ace only (or king only, if ace is turned up), and
therefore the only hints necessary are when the leader has but one
trump.

With one trump and high cards of other suits, the trump should
be led if several players remain in, but if only two or three are
standing, either of the others should be led, the higher of the two for
preference.

With one high trump and small other cards, we prefer leading the
smallest, relying on the second and third tricks for opportunities of
making our single trump. [31]

POKER.

DESCRIPTION.

The game of Poker is played with an ordinary pack of fifty-two cards.

The number of players is limited only by the number of cards, but in practice it is found better to limit each table to five, or at most six, players.

The cards have the same values as at Whist, *i.e.* ace is the highest in each suit; then follow king, queen, knave, ten, *etc.*, down to two.

In "sequences," however, the ace is the lowest card, and the king the highest.

The suit of hearts, *ceteris paribus*, takes precedence of other suits.

Before beginning play, it is customary and advisable to agree upon a sum (technically called the "limit" or "rise") which shall be the maximum stake permitted to be made by a player at one time; or, in other words, which shall be the greatest sum by which he may increase the stake at any one time.

The "limit," of course, does not refer to the total amount of a player's stakes, and it is understood that a player may stake *less* than the limit at any time, but not *more*.

After being seated, the players cut for the deal, and the player who cuts the lowest card deals first. If two or more players cut equal lowest cards, these players must cut again for the deal. [32]

The duty of dealing in each game after the first, devolves upon the player to the left of the previous dealer.

Before beginning play, every player has a right to shuffle the pack; the dealer has a right to the last shuffle. After being shuffled, the pack must be cut by the player to the right of the dealer.

The player to the left of the dealer then stakes a certain fixed sum (generally small in comparison with the limit) which is called the "ante." This initial stake must in every game be laid by the player to the left of the dealer, before the cards are dealt. He is, in fact, identified with this initial stake, and is known as "ante" throughout the game.

After "ante" has staked, the player to his left, who is called No. 1, has the option of "straddling," *i.e.* of staking a sum double that of the ante. If No. 1 does not straddle the ante, no other player may do so, and the dealer proceeds to deal the cards.

If No. 1 straddle the ante, the player to his left has the same option, and may increase the straddle by the amount of the ante. This may go on round the table, each player in turn having the right to increase the straddle before the deal; but the ante may not be increased by any straddle, or by successive straddles, to an amount exceeding one-half of the limit.

To illustrate this, let us suppose the limit be two shillings and the ante be one penny. This latter sum is staked (*i.e.* placed in the middle of the table before him) by the player on the left of the dealer. No. 1 then has the right to straddle the ante, and he may stake two pence. No. 2 then has the same option, and may, if he wish, increase the straddle by one penny. When the sum staked in this way by successive players reaches one shilling (half the limit), the straddling must cease, and the cards must be dealt. [33] It should be fully understood that if No. 1 does not exercise his right to straddle, no other player may do so.

The dealer, beginning with the player at his left hand, then deals one card, face downwards, to each player (himself included) in succession, until every player has received five cards.[1]
[1] These five cards constitute the "hand," and in no case may a player have a greater or less number of cards than five.
He then places the remainder of the pack before him on the table, face downwards. After the cards have been dealt the betting before the draw begins.

If the ante has not been straddled, the player to the left of ante has the "say," and may begin the betting before the draw.

He looks at his cards, and may either —

      (a) Reject them, and elect not to play.
      (b) Accept them, and so "open the game."

If (a) he reject his cards, he throws them, face downwards, on the table, and is out of the game until the next deal.

If (b) he accept his cards, he must stake a sum at least twice the amount of ante. He may, of course, increase the ante by any sum not exceeding the limit; but it is not usual or advisable to do more than double the ante.

No. 2, who is the player on the left of No. 1, has now the same option. He looks at his cards, and may reject them without staking (throwing them, in this case, face downwards, on the table), or he may accept them and elect to take part in the game. In this latter case he must stake a sum equal to that staked by his predecessor, or he may increase this sum by an amount not exceeding the limit.

Each succeeding player, including and ending with the [34] dealer, has, in his turn, the same privilege. He must either reject his cards and not play until the next deal, or accept them and stake a sum at least equal to that staked by his predecessor.

It is not advisable for any player to increase the stake on this first round, since to do so would probably cause succeeding players with moderate hands to reject their cards and not stake. The dealer or last player frequently, however, raises the stake with the object of inducing ante, who may hold a weak hand, to relinquish his initial stake.

Ante is the last to look at his cards, or in other words, has the last say.

If he pass, *i.e.* elect not to play, he throws his cards, face downwards, on the table, and retires from the game until the next deal, losing his original stake. If he accept his cards and elect to play, he must make his stake at least equal to that of the player on his right.

If the ante has been straddled, the player to the left of the straddler (or of the last straddler, if there be more than one) has the say, *i.e.* has the option of beginning the betting before the draw. He may, after looking at his cards, either

> (a) Throw them, face downwards, on the table, and elect
> not to play.
> (b) Accept them and "open the game."

If he open the game, he must stake a sum at least equal to double the ante and straddles together, and he may also, if he choose, stake a further sum not exceeding the limit. Whichever he elect to do, the say afterwards passes to the player at his left hand, who has a similar option; and so on round the table. The last straddler has thus the last say.

Beginning with ante, or with the first player on the left of the dealer, each player may then exchange all or any number of the cards he holds for others from the remainder [35] of the pack. He must first throw on the table, face downwards, the number of cards he wishes to exchange (this is called "discarding"), and the dealer then gives him an equal number from the top of the pack. Before exchanging any of his cards, however, each player must make his stake equal to that of ante, or of the last player.

It is not compulsory for a player to exchange all or any of his cards; but he must exercise or relinquish the privilege of doing so when his turn comes, once for all; and he cannot afterwards modify his choice, nor take back any card or cards he may have discarded.

Whether he exchange any of his cards, or whether he retains the hand first dealt out to him, each player must make his stake equal to that of ante, or of the last player, so that when all players have been supplied with, or refused, new cards, the stakes are all equal, and are all placed in the pool.

———

To give a practical illustration of this process, let us suppose that there are five players taking part in the game, that the ante is fixed at threepence, and the limit at a shilling. The players cut for deal, and the deal falls to *A*.

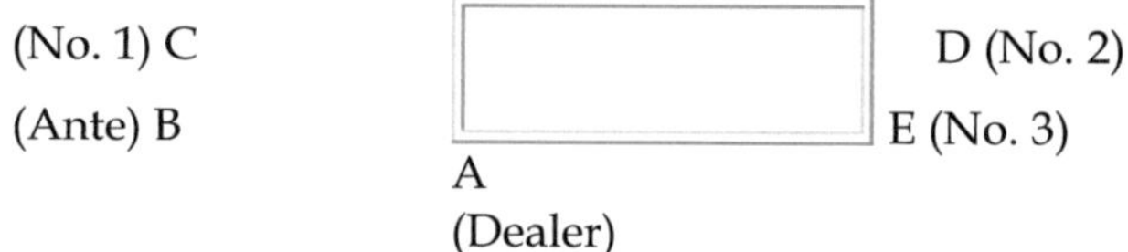

B then is ante, *C* No. 1, *etc.*

B (ante) stakes threepence. [36]

C, who has the right to straddle the ante does not do so, so no other player may.

A then deals five rounds of one card each to each player, beginning with *B*, and then puts the remainder of the pack on the table.

C (No. 1) then looks at his cards, elects to play, and stakes sixpence (double ante's stake).

D (No. 2) looks at his cards, rejects them, throwing them face downwards on the table, and retiring from the game until the next deal.

E (No. 3) looks at his cards, elects to play, and stakes sixpence.

A (dealer) looks at his cards, elects to play, and stakes one shilling and sixpence (he must stake sixpence, but he raises the stakes by the maximum amount allowed).

B (ante) looks at his cards, elects to play, and stakes one shilling and threepence, making his stake equal to *A's*. *B* then discards two of his cards, places them face downwards on the table, and receives from *A* two in their place.

C (No. 1) adds a shilling to his stake, making it equal to *A's* and *B's*, and throws down all his cards, receiving five new ones in their place.

E (No. 3), rather than increase his stake to one shilling and sixpence, relinquishes his hand, throwing down his cards, and losing the sixpence he has already staked.

A (dealer), who has already staked one shilling and sixpence, throws down one card and takes another in its place from the top of the pack.

There are now three players, *A*, *B*, and *C*, each of whom has staked one shilling and sixpence on his hand, and there is a sum of five shillings, including *E's* first stake in the pool.

No. 1 then begins play by betting a sum not exceeding [37] the limit. He may, if he choose, "stand," decline to bet until the next round, or he may throw his cards face downwards on the table and retire from the game, losing the money he has already staked. The turn then passes to No. 2. Let us suppose, in the first place, that he does bet.

The next player on his left must then —
(*a*) Make his stake equal to that of No. 1, in which case he is said to "call" No. 1, and he has the right to see No. 1's hand when the game is over, or —
(*b*) Make his stake greater than that of No. 1 by a sum not exceeding the limit, in which case he is said to "raise" No. 1; or —
(*c*) Resign the game, place his cards face downwards on the table, and lose the sum he has already staked.

Each player in succession has a similar choice. He must —
(*a*) Call the preceding player; or
(*b*) Raise the preceding player; or
(*c*) Resign his stake and the game.

If No. 1 had "stood," *i.e.* not bet when it was first his turn to play, he would have to do so when the turn came round to him again, or else relinquish his cards and his stake.

When all the stakes are equal, each player throws his cards face upwards on the table, and the player with the best hand takes the pool and all the stakes.

It will be seen thus that there is no play of the cards in Poker, as in most other card games. The best hand exposed wins the game and takes the stakes; and the play of the game consists in estimating the probable value of the opponents' hands as compared with the player's own hand. [38]

To resume our illustration (page 36).

C begins play by betting sixpence.

A also bets sixpence, making his stake equal to C's, and by doing so is said to call C.

B bets one shilling and sixpence, *i.e.* raises C a shilling. He makes his stake equal to C's and A's, and has exercised his right to increase it by a sum not exceeding the limit.

C, whose turn it now is again, adds two shillings to his stake, raising B a shilling.

A will not stake more, so relinquishes the game and his stake, placing his cards face downwards on the table.

B adds one shilling to his stake, making it equal to *C's*, and *C* is therefore compelled to show his hand. It happens to be better than *B's*, so *C* claims *B's* stake (two shillings and sixpence) and the pool (five shillings and sixpence); and the game is over.

VALUE OF THE "HANDS."

The "hands" at Poker are as follows, in order of value:—

No. 1. *Sequence Flush*, or *Straight Flush.*—A sequence of five cards of the same suit. In sequences the ace is the lowest card, and therefore ace to five is the lowest possible sequence. Nine to king is the highest possible sequence, and if a "flush," *i.e.* all the cards of the same suit, is the best possible hand in Poker.

No. 2. *Fours*, or *Four of a kind.*—Four cards of equal value, and one other card of no value. Four aces take precedence, then four kings, *etc.*

No. 3. *Full Hand.*—Three cards of equal value, and two [39] cards of equal value (for instance, three queens and two aces). The relative values of two or more "full hands" are fixed by the threes they contain, the highest three taking precedence, without regard to the value of the other two cards. Thus, a "full hand" consisting of three tens and two fours, is better than a "full hand" consisting of three nines and two kings.

No. 4. *Flush.*—Five cards of one suit. The relative values of two or more "flush" hands depend upon the value of the cards they comprise,—the highest card taking precedence.

No. 5. *Sequence*, or *Straight.* — A sequence in value of cards, not being all of one suit. Nine to king is the highest sequence, and wins, of course, against any lower sequence.

No. 6. *Triplets*, or *Threes.* — Three cards of the same value, and two other cards which are of no value. Three aces are highest, then three kings, three queens, *etc.*

No. 7. *Two Pairs.* — Two sets of two cards each, of equal value (*i.e.* 2 knaves and 2 fours for instance), and one card of no value. The relative values of two or more "two pair" hands is decided by the highest pair. If two hands have equally high pairs, the value is decided by the second pair.

No. 8. *A Pair.* — Two cards of equal value, and three of no value. Two aces are the highest pair.

If, when the cards are exposed after a game, no player holds any of the foregoing "hands," the player whose hand contains the card highest in value wins the stakes. If two or more players hold cards equally high in value, the player who holds the next highest card wins. [40]

THE JACK-POT.

If all the players reject their cards, declining to play, ante's stake remains in the pool; and the deal passes to him. Before he deals, however, he and every other player must put into the pool a sum equal to the ante. The next hand is called a Jack-pot, and the game cannot be opened by any player unless he has at least a pair of knaves in his hand. Any better hand entitles him to open the game of course, but he must have at least two knaves. If there be no players in a Jack-pot, the stakes still remain in the pool, every player again puts in a sum equal to the ante, and the deal passes on as before. In this second Jack-pot, however, two queens is the lowest hand with which the game may be opened. If there are again no players, the pool is again replenished, and the next game cannot be opened with anything less than two kings; then the Jack-pot comes down to two knaves again, and continues the same series of minimum hands—2 knaves, 2 queens, 2 kings—until the game is opened by a player holding the requisite or a better hand. A Jack-pot having been opened, the winner takes the accumulated pool, and the succeeding game reverts to the ordinary conditions, *i.e.* may be opened by any player in his turn and without reference to his hand. If a player open a Jack-pot, and all the other players pass, he must, before he can claim the pool, show, by laying his cards face upwards on the table, that he really does possess the minimum hand necessary to open the game with. If he have the minimum hand, or better, he takes the pool; but if he have not, the next game is a Jack-pot, just as if the previous game had not been opened, and the player who opened the game improperly must pay a sum double that of the ante into the pool as a penalty. [41]

MODIFICATIONS.

Modifications of the game have been from time to time introduced, but few have any claim to permanence or popularity. The best known in this country are the Blaze and the Joker.

The Blaze is an additional hand which consists of five court cards. It takes precedence of two pairs, but is beaten by triplets. The relative values of two or more blaze hands are fixed by the highest card, a hand containing ace or aces being best.

The Joker is an additional card, sometimes included in the pack, and to which any value may be given by the player holding it. If for instance, a player hold king, queen, knave, and ten of hearts, and the joker, he may call the joker ace of hearts, and so claim a sequence flush. The joker is a higher card, moreover, than the actual card whose name it takes, *i.e.* a joker which is called the king of spades is better than the real king of spades.

For convenience of reference we annex explanations of the few technical terms used in Poker.

Age.—The eldest hand, *i.e.* the player to the left of the dealer. Generally called the ante-man or "ante."

Ante.—The first stake in the game. It must be made before the cards have been dealt, by the player on the left of the dealer. It is the only compulsory stake, and for this reason the amount is fixed, and is generally small. It must not exceed one half the limit.

The player to the left of the dealer is identified with his stake, and is familiarly called ante. [42]

Bluff.—To stake an unwarrantable sum on a weak hand for the purpose of inducing the other players to relinquish their stakes rather than continue betting. To pretend to have a good hand.

Blaze.—A hand consisting of five court cards (see p. 41).

Chips.—Counters. An American term, little used by English players. *To chip* means to stake chips, to bet.

Call.—To call the preceding player is to stake an amount equal to his stake (see p. 37).

Discard.—To throw away cards so as to receive others in exchange for them (see p. 35).

Draw.—To receive cards from the dealer in exchange for an equal number discarded.

Eldest Hand.—The player to the left of the dealer. See *Ante.*

Foul Hand.—A hand containing more or less than five cards. Such hand must be relinquished, and the owner must retire from that game, losing any sum he may have staked.

Go Better.—See *Raise.*

Go in.—To stake a sum equal to double the ante and any straddles or raises which may have been added to it, in order to qualify for drawing and playing for the pool.

Hand. — The five cards held by any player.

Jack-pot. — The game which follows an unopened game, *i.e.* which follows a game in which every player had rejected his cards (see p. 40).

Joker. — An extra card, to which any value may be assigned by the player holding it (see p. 41).

Kitty. — A portion of the stakes set aside in every game, either to defray the expenses of the table, or as a reward for some specially good hand.

Limit. — The maximum amount by which stakes may be [43] increased at one time. The limit, which has a tendency to prevent wild and unreasonable betting, is generally fixed before play begins.

Make Good. — To make good is really the same as to call, but a player may make good his previous bet, *i.e.* may make it equal to that of the previous player, and may afterwards raise.

No. 1. — The player to the left of ante — the next player is No. 2, and so on round to the dealer.

Pass. — To give up the game. To throw the cards, face downwards, on the table, and cease playing until the next deal. The player who passes loses any sum he may have staked.

Pat. — A term used in reference to the hand originally dealt to each player in a game. To play pat is to bet on the hand originally dealt, without drawing. A pat hand is a hand of high value, which has been dealt to the player, a hand which he cannot hope to improve by drawing.

Player. — This is not strictly a technical term, but the tyro should note that the persons seated at the table are not necessarily all players. One or more may retire from the game, and on doing so forfeit all their interest, and cease to be players in that game. There are seldom more than two or three players remaining at the end of a game.

Pool. — The whole of the stakes in a game.

Pot. — The pool.

Raise. — To raise the preceding player is to stake a sum in excess of that staked by him.

Rise. — See *Limit.*

Say. — The option, which comes to each player in turn, of playing, and therefore betting, or of passing, *i.e.* throwing down his cards and resigning the game.

See. — To see or call your opponent is to make your [44] stake equal to his. If the stake be not then raised by succeeding players, every hand must be exposed (see p. 37).

Show. — The exposure of a hand or hands at the end of the game.

Skip Straight or Skip Sequence. — A sequence of alternate cards — two, four, six, eight, ten, for instance. This hand is sometimes introduced, and takes precedence of *triplets.* It is beaten by an ordinary sequence.

Straddle. — To raise the ante. To double the initial stake made by ante in every game before the cards are dealt. Straddling the ante gives the straddler (or the last straddler, if there be more than one) the advantage of the last say before the draw.

Straight. — A sequence, a series of five cards in regular order (see p. 38).

THE STAKES.

As before stated, the ante and limit should be fixed before play begins, and once fixed should not be altered in any circumstances. Players who have lost sometimes apply to have the limit raised. This should be refused.

The ante should be a small sum, the smaller the better. It must not exceed half the limit, and for general play a much lower proportion is desirable. If the limit be one shilling, the ante may be fixed at one penny.

Counters are desirable for play in all cases; they are in every way more convenient, and avoid the constant trouble of giving change.

They should be circular in form, and all of one size, but of three values, represented by different colours: —

1, say Red; the value of ante.

2, say White; treble the value of ante.

3, say Blue; the value of the limit. [45]
The counters should be sold to each player before the game begins, and be bought back at the same rate after play.

HINTS TO PLAYERS.

A few words of advice to the tyro may not, in conclusion, be out of place. They will not make him into a good player — practice and experience alone can do that, — but they may prevent him paying for his experience more than is necessary: —

Do not play with folk you do not know.

Never play with a man you cannot implicitly trust. The game needs all your attention, and it becomes a toil instead of a pleasure if you have to be on the watch for unfair play.

Never play for a stake you are not prepared to lose.

Fix a limit to your losses and cease play at once when they reach it. The temptation to continue is greater when losing than when winning.

Fix a time to cease play — and keep to it.

Perfect self-control is, it is needless to say, essential to successful play.

The man whose losses make him ill-tempered, must not play at all. He certainly cannot win, since loss of temper involves loss of judgment. A game like Poker, which it must be confessed is not calculated to rouse the finer feelings of humanity, is only tolerable when played under the severest self-imposed restraint.

Avoid playing, moreover, with an opponent who cannot keep his temper. You will beat him, no doubt, but anger is infectious, and, unless you are blessed with extraordinary self-command, the risk of catching it is too great.

Neither voice, manner, nor features should give the [46] slightest clue to your hand. One or other will do so at first inevitably, and all will need a constant effort to control. The perfect Poker player sits like an automaton, and his face is a mask.

Study your opponents, their features and manner, in success and failure. To an accurate observer they will generally betray themselves. An American authority says, "the study of my adversaries is, of more value than the study of my cards."

Bluffing is at best a very dangerous game, seldom worth the risk, and it involves, even for its occasional success, a very just estimate of your opponents. Remember that you cannot bluff even a tyro out of "fours."

If you do bluff, bluff when you are winning, and have established a fear of your hands in the minds of your opponents.

To bluff when losing is insanity.

In actual play there are few maxims which hold good for all cases. All depends on what is termed luck, and nearly every Poker player recognises luck, whatever that may be, as an important factor in the game—one they often allow to override calculable chances. Some players seem to have almost persistent good luck, and win with comparatively poor hands. Others are just as unlucky, losing with high cards.

With a pair, if you decide to play, discard the remaining three cards. You have then three chances of triplets.

With triplets discard one, your chance of getting fours is remote, and you leave your opponents in doubt as to whether you are not trying for a flush.

With triplets you may generally risk *seeing* your opponent.

Never try for the completing card of a sequence. If, for instance, you have 3, 4, 6, 7 and king, do not play—[47] discarding the king on the chance of receiving a 5. Throw up your hand. With a sequence you may generally wait till your opponents think fit to see you.

With fours, discard the odd card, in order to mislead your opponents. This hand, or anything better, so seldom comes to a player, that he is justified in staking as much as possible upon it.

Be content to pass sometimes with the better hand. The best players do so, since it costs less than the habit of calling.

Neither borrow nor lend a penny at the table.

RULES OF THE GAME.

The Deal.

1. The cards shall be the ordinary pack of fifty-two cards.

2. The players, after being seated, shall each draw a card from the pack, face downwards, and the player drawing the card lowest in value (ace being lowest), shall deal in the first game. If two or more players draw cards of equal value, such cards being the lowest, such players only shall draw again for the deal.

3. Any player may demand to shuffle the cards, but the dealer shall have a right to the last shuffle before the cards are cut.

4. The pack shall be shuffled by the dealer, and cut by the player on the right of the dealer, before every deal.

5. The cards shall be shuffled, face downwards, above the table.

6. The cards shall be dealt, face downwards, so that their faces cannot be seen; and they must be placed by the dealer on the table in front of the players to whom they are severally dealt. [48]

7. The dealer shall give one card from the top of the pack to each player in turn from right to left, beginning with the player at his left hand, and in this order shall give to each player five cards.

8. If the cards be dealt without the pack having been cut, and if the fact be pointed out to the dealer before the deal is finished, it is a misdeal, and there shall be a new deal by the same dealer.

9. If the fact that the cards have been dealt without the pack having been cut for such deal be not pointed out to the dealer before such deal is finished, the deal shall stand.

10. If a card be found face upwards in the pack before the deal is finished, it is a misdeal, and there shall be a new deal by the same dealer.

11. If the dealer, while dealing, accidentally expose a card, such card shall be accepted by the player to whom it is dealt, as though it had not been exposed, and the dealer shall not, nor shall any player, exchange such exposed card for another, except in the regular course of discarding after the deal is completed.

12. If any player have more or less than five cards dealt to him, and if such player, or any player, announce the fact before the cards are raised from the table, it is a misdeal, and there shall be a new deal by the same dealer.

13. If any player have more or less than five cards dealt to him, and if the fact be not announced before any portion of the hand is raised from the table, such hand is a foul hand, and the player to whom it is dealt shall place his cards, face downwards, on the table, and retire from the game, and shall forfeit his stake in that game.

14. If a player be compelled to retire from the game in consequence of having a foul hand dealt to him, his stake, [49] if he has staked, shall remain in the pool, and the dealer shall refund such player the amount of his ante or straddle only in that game.

15. No player shall speak to the dealer while the cards are being dealt..

16. If any player speak to the dealer, or distract him by noise or gesture, while the cards are being dealt, such player, and not the dealer, shall refund, as provided by Rule 14, the ante or straddle of any player to whom a foul hand is dealt in that deal.

17. The deal shall be finished when every player has received five cards.

18. The duty of dealing shall devolve upon each player in turn, from right to left; the player to the left of the last dealer shall be the dealer in the next game. If the dealer in a game pass and retire, he shall continue his duty as dealer in that game.

19. The ante shall not exceed one-half the amount of the limit.

20. The ante shall be staked by the player to the left of the dealer before the cards are dealt.

21. The right to straddle shall belong to the player to the left of ante. If he does not straddle, no other player shall, do so; but if he does straddle, the succeeding players shall have, in turn from right to left, and ending with the dealer, the right to increase the straddle in every case by the amount of the ante.

22. The ante shall not be straddled by a player, or by successive players, to an amount exceeding one-half the limit.

23. If the ante be not straddled, the player to the left of [50] ante shall have first say after the deal, and ante shall have the last say.

24. If the ante be straddled, the player to the left of the straddler (or of the last straddler, if there be more than one) shall have first say after the deal, and the last straddler shall have the last say.

The Play.

25. The turn to say shall pads from right to left, and the player who has first say after the deal shall, if he open the game, stake a sum at least double the amount of ante.

26. Each succeeding player shall, if he play, at least make good his stake to that of the preceding player.

27. If a player pass, he shall place his cards, face downwards, on the table, and shall not again take them into his hand, and he shall forfeit unconditionally his stake and his right to play in that game.

28. A player who retires from the game shall not divulge the cards nor the value of the hand he has thrown down.

29. If the game be not opened by any player, the ante and straddles, if any, shall remain in the pool, and the next game shall be a Jack-pot.

30. In a Jack-pot every player shall pay into the pool a sum equal to the ante, and the game shall not be opened by any player unless he have two knaves, or better, in his original hand.

31. If a Jack-pot be not opened by any player, each player shall again pay into the pool a sum equal to the ante, and the next game shall be a Jack-pot, and shall not be opened by any player unless he have two queens, or better, in his original hand. [51]

32. A third successive Jack-pot shall not be opened with less than two kings, and for successive Jack-pots the series of two knaves, two queens, two kings shall be maintained as the minimum hands with which the games may severally be opened.

33. If a player open a Jack-pot and win the stakes, he shall show his hand (notwithstanding any law which in ordinary circumstances permits him to keep it concealed) before he shall claim the pool; and if he have not two knaves, or the minimum hand with which the game may be opened according to the above laws, or a better hand, he shall not claim the pool, and he shall pay into the pool, as penalty, a sum equal to double the ante, and the next game shall be a Jack-pot as if the previous game had not been opened.

The Draw.

34. The first player to the left of the dealer shall have first draw.

35. The turn to draw shall pass from right to left.

36. Before drawing any card or cards, a player shall make his stake equal to the highest stake on the table, and he shall discard as many cards, and no more, as he intends to draw.

37. Cards discarded shall be placed on the table, face downwards, and shall not again be taken into the hand of the player discarding them.

38. If a player, when it is his turn to draw, do not discard or have not discarded, he shall forfeit his right to discard and draw in that game.

39. Each player, after discarding, shall ask for the same number of cards he has discarded, and the dealer shall place on the table, in front of such player, such number of cards, face downwards, from the top of the pack. [52]

40. If the dealer, in giving to any player the number of cards demanded after the discard, expose a card or cards; such exposed card or cards shall be returned to the pack, and shall not be given to the player.

41. If the dealer have not sufficient cards remaining in the pack to give to every player the number of cards demanded after the discard, the dealer shall call upon any player who has not discarded, but who intends to discard, to do so, and to announce the number he discards, and the dealer also shall discard, and the dealer (or some player for him) shall then collect the whole of the cards discarded, and shall collect them in a pack and shuffle them, and shall have them cut by the player at his right hand, and shall then use them to supply the players who have discarded.

42. If the dealer give to any player more than the number of cards demanded by such player, and such player or any player point out the excess before any of the cards so given are raised from the table, the dealer shall take back and return to the pack the card or cards given in excess of the number demanded.

43. If the dealer give to any player less than the number of cards demanded by such player, the dealer shall make good such deficiency if it be pointed out by any player before the cards already given have been raised from the table.

44. If a player demand a greater or less number of cards than he has discarded, the dealer need not give him such wrong number, but may demand to see how many cards have been discarded, and give him that number.

45. If the dealer give to a player the number of cards demanded by such player, and such number prove to be more or less than the number of cards discarded, the hand of such player shall be a foul

hand, whether it be raised from [53] the table or not, and such player shall retire from the game and forfeit his stake in that game.

46. It there be a dispute between a player and the dealer, as to the number of cards demanded, the evidence of the person at the left hand of the dealer (whether he be playing in that game or have retired) shall be taken as deciding the matter; and if the person at the left hand of the dealer cannot give evidence, or if he be the player who is disputing with the dealer, the evidence of the person to the right of the dealer shall be taken, and shall be held conclusive, and if the person to the right of the dealer cannot give evidence, the evidence of the first person (beginning with the first person to the left of the disputing player, and going in succession to each person from right to left) who can give evidence, shall be taken as conclusive; and if no person at the table can give evidence, the disputing player shall be held to have demanded the proper number of cards.

47. If the dealer draw more or less than the number of cards he has discarded, he shall be held to have demanded such improper number, and his hand shall be a foul hand, and he shall retire from the game and shall forfeit his state in that game.

48. If cards drawn be raised from the table, and the hand be found to contain more or less than five cards, such hand shall be a foul hand, and the player to whom it belongs shall retire from the game and shall forfeit his stake in that game.

49. Any player after drawing, but before raising his hand from the table, may ask the dealer how many cards he, the dealer, drew, and the dealer shall answer correctly.

50. If a player raise from the table the cards he has drawn, or if he bet, he shall forfeit his right to ask the dealer how many cards he, the dealer, drew. [54]

51. The dealer shall not give any information as to the number of cards drawn by any other player.

The Betting.

52. All bets shall be deposited in the pool.

53. The first player to the left of the ante shall have first right to bet after the draw, whether the ante-man have retired or not. The turn to bet shall pass to each player from right to left, and each player shall stake a sum at least equal to that staked by the preceding player.

54. If, when his turn comes, any player have not staked, and does not stake a sum at least equal to that staked by the preceding player, such player shall place his cards, face downwards, on the table, and shall retire from the game, and shall forfeit his stake in that game.

55. A bet once made, whether made in proper turn or not, cannot be recalled.

56. A bet[1] is complete and irrevocable when the player making it has deposited the amount in money or value on the table, and such deposit shall be considered as a deposit into the pool.
[1] *i.e.:* The bet is the actual amount deposited, and the player's statement that he intends or intended depositing another amount is of no value.

57. The statement of his intention to bet, or to refrain from betting, shall not invalidate the right of any player to bet or pass when his turn comes.

58. If a player bet or raise the stake of a previous player, and no other player call or raise him, such player wins the pool, and shall not be compelled to show his hand.

59. When the bets of all the players are equal, each player in turn, beginning with the player to the left of the [55] last player, shall show his hand, and the player with the best hand shall win the pool.

60. If a player's bet be raised, and such player have not funds to call the raise, he may deposit in the pool whatever funds he has, and demand a show for that amount. If, when the game is over, he prove to hold the best hand, he shall claim from the pool the amount of the ante and straddle or straddles (if any), and also a sum equal to his stake from every player in the game at the time of his demanding a show, out of their stakes. The holder of the next best hand shall claim the remainder of the pool.

61. A player demanding a show for a certain sum under the above rule, shall not stop the game if there be other players who wish to continue the betting, and he shall not show his hand until the game is over.

62. If a player borrow money to raise, he shall borrow to call.

63. If a player bet with a foul hand, he shall lose his stake.

64. If any player be found to have a foul hand at the end of the game, he shall forfeit his stake; and if there be only one other player, that player shall claim the pool; and if there be more than one other player, the holder of the best hand shall claim the pool.

The Hands.

65. The following shall be the hands in order of value; the first being the highest:—1, Sequence flush; 2, Fours; 3, Full; 4, Flush; 5, Sequence not a flush; 6, Threes; 7, Two pairs; 8, A pair.

66. If there be two or more flush sequences shown, the player whose sequence contains the highest card (ace being the lowest) shall be held to have the best hand. [56]

67. If there be two or more fours shown, fours being the best hand, the player who has the four cards highest in value shall be held to have the best hand.

68. If there be two or more full hands shown, a full hand being the best hand, the player whose full hand contains threes highest in value shall be held to have the best hand.

69. If there be two or more flush hands shown, a flush hand being the best hand, a flush in hearts shall be held to be the best hand; and if there be no flush hand in hearts, the flush hand which contains the card highest in value, and which is not tied by a card of equal value in another flush hand, shall be the best hand.

70. If there be two or more sequences shown, a sequence being the best hand, the player whose sequence contains the highest card (ace being the lowest) shall be held to be the best hand; and if there be two or more sequences of cards of equal value, a sequence in hearts, *ceteris paribus*, shall be the best hand.

71. The ace shall only begin a sequence; it shall not end a sequence after a king, nor shall it be an intermediate card between a king and a two.[1]

[1] This law, and the others which are involved in it, has only the authority of custom in this country. Some American writers permit of the ace being used at the beginning or end of a sequence, making ten to ace the highest sequence.

72. If there be two or more threes shown, threes being the best hand, the hand containing the threes highest in value shall be the best hand.

73. If there be two or more two-pairs shown, two-pairs being the best hand, the hand containing the pair highest in value shall be the best hand; and if two two-pair hands contain pairs equally high in value, such pairs being the [57] highest, the value of the other pair shall decide which is the better hand.

74. If there be two or more pairs, pairs being the best hand, the hand containing the pair highest in value shall be the best hand; and if two hands contain equally high pairs, the hand containing the highest card which is not tied by an equally high card in the other hand shall be the better hand.

75. If no pair hand nor any better hand be shown, the player whose hand contains the card highest in value which is not tied by a card of similar value in another competing hand, shall be held to have the best hand.

76. If, when the final call is made and the hands shown, two or more players hold hands identical in value, such players shall share the pool equally between them.

Disputes.

77. Any dispute shall be referred to the dealer, unless he be one of the disputing persons; and if on a matter of fact his decision shall be final and binding; and if on a matter of law, he shall interpret these laws literally, and not by implication.

78. If the dealer be one of the disputing persons, the dispute shall be referred to the person on the left of the dealer, and if he be one of the disputing persons, it shall be referred to the person on the tight of the dealer.

79. In a dispute, the dealer, or any player appointed to settle such dispute, may appeal to any person at the table for evidence, and if such person can give evidence, he shall do so.

80. If the players agree to waive a particular rule on a particular occasion, a like concession cannot be claimed on another similar occasion. [58]

81. These rules shall be binding on all players, unless a departure from them has been agreed upon unanimously before play begins, and if one or more rules he abrogated by common consent, such abrogation shall hold only for that sitting, and for that sitting only so long as there is no change of players, and it shall not apply to any future sitting. [59]

VINGT-UN.

Vingt-un, or twenty-one, is another game we find described in books published at the commencement of the present century. Its name would seem to imply that it is of French origin; but in reference to this, as well as in regard to the date of its introduction into the country, we have no definite details. The manner of playing it at the present time is very little different from that practised at the earlier date mentioned, although modifications have been introduced in some minor points, and the tendency is to make yet further departures from the methods adopted in years gone by.

The game is well suited for a large number of players, and may also be engaged in by smaller parties; its practice, with even only two competing, being both interesting and exciting. It is purely a game of chance, and little or no skill is required in playing it, although a little judgment may often prove of advantage to the player who exercises it.

Vingt-un is played with an ordinary pack of fifty-two cards, which count in accordance with the number of pips on each, the ace reckoning as either one or eleven, at the option of the player, and each of the court cards counting ten. No distinction is made during any part of the game in the various suits, each of the four sorts being of equal value in counting the points.

A player may retire after the completion of any hand, [60] and the game itself may be concluded at the same period, although it is desirable to arrive at some understanding, previous to the commencement of play, as to the method to be adopted in closing it, as, from the fact of the deal being an advantage, it is unfair to conclude until each of those engaged has had a turn, or equal number of turns, as dealer. This is assuming that the deal goes round in rotation, which is the arrangement now generally adopted, in lieu of the old-fashioned method of transferring the privilege to the player throwing the dealer out by the declaration of a "natural" Vingt-un, as explained later on. It must be understood, however, that with several players engaged it may take a considerable time for the deal to pass round, unless it be further agreed that each player shall hold the deal for a limited period, another modification, and one possessing many advantages over the old system, which was, in reality, a mere question of chance, and often resulted in the privilege of dealing being very unevenly divided among those engaged in play.

As already mentioned, the deal is an advantage, and the earliest consideration should be to decide who is first to enjoy the privilege, and for how long. By the old system one player retained the deal until put out by one of the others receiving a natural Vingt-un, that is, an ace (counting as 11) and a 10, or court card (counting as 10), and, as a consequence, the deal often remained for a considerable period with the same person, to the disadvantage of all the others engaged in the game; and even when a change was made, it was not in any definite order, but by mere chance, governed by the fall of the cards.

Modern innovations in the method of playing the game have tended to remove these objections, — firstly, by arranging that the deal shall pass in regular order from left to right; [61] and secondly, by placing a limit on the number of rounds to be dealt by each player in turn. Although the latter of these changes is not yet generally adopted, the former is almost universal; and we shall now proceed to explain the game on that basis, ignoring the second point, for the time being, as, although its adoption may make matters more equal, it has, perhaps, the disadvantage of depriving the game of one of its main elements of chance, and, in the opinion of many, thereby robs it of much of its attractiveness.

The limits of the stakes are first determined, and then the dealer is decided upon. The minimum is usually one coin or counter, and the maximum whatever may be agreed upon. The maximum is understood to mean the highest amount that may be staked by a player on his card, and not the maximum that may be lost or won over any hand, for, by the rules of the game, the dealer is allowed to double the stakes, even if a player has staked the maximum. If after that any one secures a Vingt-un, *i.e* twenty-one points, that again doubles the stakes, and thus it is quite possible for a player to win or lose four times the amount of the maximum over one hand.

The object of the players is to secure from their cards — the pips on which count as already mentioned — twenty-one points, or as near that number as possible; hence the title. During the progress of the game the dealer pays those players who secure better hands than his own, and receives from all who over-draw, or whose points are lower or equal to his, the only exception being in the case of a tie with a natural Vingt-un, when neither the holder nor the dealer pays anything to the other, the tie in such a case [62] simply nullifying matters between the two. If the dealer over-draws, he only pays to those who are standing in, and does not return anything to those players who have paid him on their over-drawing; and herein lies the main advantage of the deal, for, as will be found in practice, the majority of hands are decided by over-drawing, which must necessarily be to the benefit of the dealer.

The dealer having been decided upon, takes the pack of cards and shuffles them, after which he has the pack cut by the player on his right-hand side, and then proceeds to distribute one card, face downwards and unexposed, to each player, dealing in regular order from left to right.

Each player, in turn, looks at his card, and stakes on it whatever amount he chooses — which he usually does by placing coins or counters in front of him. In deciding on the amount of his stake, a player is guided by the chance he considers the card gives him of ultimately making twenty-one, or a near approach thereto. When it comes round to the dealer's turn, he also looks at his card, but does not stake anything upon it; he may, however, if he considers his card a good one, double the stakes of the other players, which he does by calling "double." In that case the individual players add the "double" to their stake, and the amounts being thus settled all round, the dealer gives a second card to each player, in the same order as the first, and also unexposed. The dealer then looks at his own two cards, and if he should have received a natural Vingt-un, he at once declares it; throws the two cards, face upwards, on the table, and collects the stakes from the other players, the amount in this case being double from each, as the result of the Vingt-un; so that, if the dealer had previously doubled, as he probably would have done when he found his first card was an ace or a 10 (or court card), [63] he would collect four times the amount staked by each o the players on their original card. The only exception to this is in the case of a player who, like the dealer, has received a natural Vingt-un—in that case neither pays to the other, as previously mentioned.

If either of the players other than the dealer should receive a natural Vingt-un, he should at once declare it, and claim double the amount of his stake, or of the double, if that was called, from the dealer, who is thereupon deprived of his privilege of dealing, the right of continuing the deal passing to the player on his left-hand side.—It is often agreed that a natural shall not throw out the dealer, and in some cases the holder of a natural receives a stake from each of the other players. (*See* Variations in regard to the two points.)

If the dealer has not secured a natural Vingt-un, he turns to the player on his left, and, if that player desires it, he gives him—face upwards, and from off the top of the remainder of the pack—a third, fourth, or fifth card; in fact, as many more as may be required by the player, until he considers it safe to stand, or has over-drawn, *i.e.*, got beyond the 21 points. For instance, suppose a player receives at first a 4, and then a 9, making 13; he asks for a third card, and may receive a 7, making his total 20, on which he would stand. Had his third card been a 9, it would have been an over-draw, and the player would have had to pay the dealer the amount he staked, or the double, if the dealer had doubled. At the same time he would throw up his cards, or hand them to the player on the dealer's right, who is termed the pone, and whose duty it is to collect the cards as they are played and keep them in readiness for the dealer when he requires a further supply. A player when throwing up his cards must not expose the two first dealt [64] to him, neither may the pone or either of the other players look at them.

Having settled with the player on his left, the dealer goes to the next in order, and treats him in a similar manner, and so on, until he has gone the round of the table. He then turns up his own two cards in front of him, and in view of the company, and decides, as the others have done, as to whether he will stand on the two he has, or take a further card or cards. If he decides to stand on the two he already has, he calls on those players who have not over-drawn to declare their hands, and each in turn does so, the dealer receiving the stakes when his points are higher or are equal to those of the other players, and paying when his points are lower than theirs. If he elects to take a third card, he deals it from the top of the pack; and if the third card does not satisfy him, he may take more; when satisfied, he challenges the others, as just explained. If, however, he over-draws, he pays to all who are standing, but not to those who have previously over-drawn and thrown up.

If the dealer should succeed in securing such cards (other than an ace and 10) as to make exactly 21 points—a "drawn" Vingt-un—he receives double stakes from each of the players, excepting those who have also drawn a Vingt-un, who only pay the amount staked; and those who have previously over-drawn and thrown up, who do not have to pay anything further. If a player has a drawn Vingt-un and the dealer has not, or the dealer has over-drawn, then the dealer has to pay the holder of the Vingt-un double the amount of his stake, or of the double if that has been called.

Should any of the players receive for the first cards two of the same denomination,—for instance, two aces, two twos, two kings, two queens, *etc.*,—he has the option of staking a [65] separate amount on each of them, but it is not compulsory that he should do so. If he decides to divide his pair, he puts on the second card a separate stake, the amount of which need not be similar to that of his original one, and then asks the dealer for two other cards with which to complete the two hands he then possesses. If either of these later cards should be of the same denomination as the first two, the player may also stand independently on that card, in which case he would, of course, have three hands, with a separate stake on each. The same opportunity would occur if he received all four of the kind—he could then play on four independent hands. This division of cards is equally available for the dealer, or all or any of the other players, so that two or more may have duplicate hands in the same round, provided they receive similar cards at the outset, for it is only when the original pairs occur in the first two cards that it is permissible to divide them; that is to say, if the third card received by any player matches either of those already in the hand, no division is allowable.

At this game the pack of cards is not re-united after each round; the dealer works with the one pack until he gets to the last card, and the pone collects the used cards as they are disposed of by the players. When the dealer comes to the last card of the pack, he does not deal it or otherwise use it as he has done with the others, but hands it, unexposed, to the pone, who adds it to those already in his care, shuffles them, and hands them to the dealer, who proceeds with the game as before.

The same procedure is repeated until one of the players secures a natural Vingt-un, which, unless the dealer also holds a natural that hand, puts the dealer out, and the deal passes, either to the next player, or to the holder of the natural, as may have been decided upon. It is, however, [66] best to adopt the former system, for the reason already given, and in that case it is often considered desirable to have a pool, which is secured by the player declaring the natural. (*See* Variations.)

There is one exception to the power of a natural Vingt-un to put the dealer out—namely, when it occurs in the first hand of the deal; then the dealer disregards it, except that he has to pay to the holder as for a drawn Vingt-un, and proceeds with his deal until a second natural occurs.

We will now amplify, as far as is necessary, the points already touched upon, and introduce the Variations recognised in connection with the game.

DEALING.

The first dealer is settled by one of the company distributing the cards in the same manner as explained in connection with "Nap" (see page 9), except that in the case of Vingt-un the player to whom the first *ace* is dealt becomes the dealer. He proceeds with the game as explained on page 61.

If, in preparing the pack for the dealer, any confusion occurs, or any card or cards are exposed, the whole pack must be re-shuffled and cut again. If two cards are dealt to one player, the error may be rectified if discovered before a third card is dealt; but if a third card has been dealt, then the player receiving the surplus card must look at his hand, and reject which of the two he chooses. If the dealer gives himself two cards at one time, and the mistake is not discovered until another card has been dealt, then the pone must take one of the cards, at random, and add it to the used portion of the pack.

A card exposed in dealing may be kept or rejected at the [67] option of the player; but if the dealer exposes one of his own cards, he must retain it.

DRAWING.

The whole of the hands having been dealt—that is, two cards given to each player, and also to cases of divided pairs, the drawing of further cards commences. The dealer begins with the player on his left-hand side, and he, if he does not require any more cards, says "content." If he does require more, he says "yes," or, "a card," when the dealer delivers one from the top of the undealt portion of the pack, placing it face upwards on the table in front of the player. If another card or cards is needed, it must be given in like manner, until the player is content or has over-drawn. The dealer must settle with one player before he attends to the next, and similarly, when a player is standing on divided pairs, he must settle with one hand before attending to the other.

If the dealer gives a player two cards while the process of drawing is going on, the player may keep either or both of them; but if he rejects one, he must be regarded as content, and cannot draw another card. The one rejected is added to the stock in the hands of the pone. If the dealer in drawing gives himself two cards, he must keep them both, and suffer the consequences of an over-draw if then his points exceed 21.

If the dealer distributes the draw cards out of order, the player or players missed may either be supplied at any time from the top of the pack, or they may throw up their cards.

If a player draws separately on his two cards, when they do not pair, he has to pay the dealer on each hand, and forfeits any amount he may have won. [68]

In any of these cases of irregularity, the offender pays a penalty to the pool, if there be one.

POOL.

A pool may be formed for any purpose that may be decided upon, and may be made up according to arrangement. For this purpose, it may be agreed (a) that each player contribute a coin or counter to the pool at the commencement of each deal; (b) that whenever the dealer over-draws, he pay a penalty to the pool; (c) that whenever the dealer receives on ties, he pay a proportion to the pool, say one-fourth or one-third of his receipts. Other methods of increasing the pool will present themselves in actual play, those here inserted being intended as specimens of what may be done, or to form a basis on which to work.

LIMITING THE DEAL.

In the game we have described we have adopted the principle that the declaration of a natural Vingt-un throws the dealer out; but another method is to limit the deal to a certain number of hands, or to allow the dealer to go through the pack twice, or to have two packs of cards shuffled together, and go through them once. In these cases the dealer is allowed to draw from the used pack as many cards as may be necessary to complete a round started upon with his limited supply, and the cards are prepared by the pone for the purpose, being all collected, shuffled, and cut before they are used by the dealer.

SELLING THE DEAL.

Should a player object to take his turn at dealing, or desire to part with it for other reason, he is at liberty to sell the right to any other player; and in view of the fact that [69] the deal is an advantage, a purchaser will generally be found. The buyer has to deal the cards, but does not change his seat. He has to commence each time with the player on the left-hand side of the proper dealer, and when the buyer loses his turn, the deal reverts to the player who would have had the next turn had there been no sale. The buyer takes his turn with the others in the ordinary course.

ADDITIONAL PRIVILEGES FOR A NATURAL.

It is sometimes agreed that the holder of a natural Vingt-un, providing the dealer has not also received a natural, shall be entitled to an amount equal to, or double that of his own stake from each of the other players, unless there be other Vingt-uns, the holders of which are exempted from payment. This is the old fashioned method of playing the game, and in many quarters the rule had been abolished, because, as the deal formerly passed to the holder of the natural Vingt-un, who threw the dealer out, that was considered sufficient reward for holding the two cards. Now, however, that the deal merely passes to the next in order, it is desirable that some further reward should follow from the best possible hand, and the payment of a stake or a double from each player appears to be the fairest method, especially as the declaration of a natural brings the deal nearer to all. The same result may be achieved by agreeing that the contents of a pool, for which provision has already been made, shall go to the player declaring the natural. [70]

COMMERCE.

DESCRIPTION OF THE GAME.

Ninety years ago the game of Commerce was recognised as being played in two distinct ways, the new and the old mode, so that it may justly be termed one of the oldest round games now practised. Although it is not so popular as some of the others treated of in this volume, it will be found to be a good game; exciting, entertaining, and well deserving of more extended popularity than it has lately enjoyed.

Commerce is usually played with the full pack of fifty-two cards, but if the number of players does not exceed seven the smaller pack of thirty-two may be used, the game being available for any number of players within the range of the pack, say seven with the thirty-two cards, and twelve with the fifty-two.

The cards count in the usual way, except that in reckoning the number of pips upon them, which is sometimes necessary in the course of play, the ace counts for eleven, and the court cards for ten each. There is no particular suit or trumps recognised in the game, the object of the players being to secure special combinations of the cards, technically termed (*a*) Tricon, (*b*) Sequence, (*c*) Flush, (*d*) Pair, (*e*) Point, which range in value in the order given. The holder of the best combination in each [71] round is the winner, and he takes the pool or whatever other stake may have been decided upon.

The five combinations just mentioned consist of the following:—

(*a*) *Tricon.*—Three cards of the same denominations as, for example, three aces, three fives, three knaves, *etc.*

(*b*) *Sequence.*—Three following cards of the same suit, as, for instance, ace, two, three; ten, knave, queen; queen, king, ace, etc. Although the ace may be used at either end to form a sequence, it must not be so used between a king and a two. King, ace, two, is not, therefore, permissible as a sequence.

(*c*) *Flush.*—Three cards of the same suit, irrespective of value.

(*d*) *Pair.* — Two cards of the same denomination, the third one being different.

(*e*) *Point.* — The total number of pips on the three cards, ace reckoning for eleven, and either of the court cards for ten.

In case of a tie between two or more of the players in any round, the following rules are observed: —

(*a*) With Tricons, the highest wins, aces being first in this respect; then kings, queens, *etc.*, down to twos.

(*b*) With Sequences, the highest wins; the ace, king, queen sequence reckoning as the best, and the three, two, ace sequence as the lowest.

(*c*) With Flushes, the one making the best "point" — as already described — wins.

(*d*) With Pairs, the highest wins. If two players are alike, then the holder of the highest third card has the preference.

(*e*) With Point a tie is very rare; but if equality does [72] occur, then the holder of the first highest card different from the opponent's wins.

The deal is an advantage, and on that account it is best, when a finish is desired, to conclude the game just before the first dealer's turn comes round again, as then all the players will have had an equal number of deals. Should it be found necessary, however, to conclude before the original dealer's turn, play may be discontinued after the completion of any deal, although such a course is somewhat unfair to the intervening players.

There is only one stake recognised in the game, so that it is simply necessary to decide what shall be regarded as the value of a counter, or what coin shall constitute the limit.

The amount of the stake having been settled, the dealer is decided upon in the same manner as described in connection with the game of "Nap" (see page 9). Each of the players then pays the amount of the stake into the pool, the dealer also contributing on account of his deal, so that he has to pay double.

The pack having been shuffled by the dealer, and cut by the player on his right-hand side, three cards are distributed to each player, face downwards and unexposed. The cards may be dealt either singly or all three at a time, at the option of the dealer. The players having looked at their cards, the dealer first addresses the one on his left-hand side, and asks if he will trade; and he must either do so or stand on the cards dealt him.

If he decides to stand on the cards he has received, he turns his hand face upwards on the table, and all the other players do the same, when the holder of the best hand takes the amount in the pool, and also receives the amount of a stake from the dealer, who is thus penalised for the [73] advantage that accrues to him from selling cards to those who wish to trade for ready money, the amount he receives on that account becoming his own property, subject to the payment mentioned. Should the player who declares to stand be beaten by any of the others, he has to pay an additional stake to the holders of the better hands.

If the player decides to trade, he may either do so for "ready money" or by "barter." If for ready money, he continues operations with the dealer; if by barter, with the next player in order round the table, who, in turn, must exchange a card, unless he has a hand sufficiently strong to stand upon, in which case he at once declares it.

If the player trades for ready money, he throws out a card from his hand, pays a stake to the dealer, and receives the top card from the pack; his rejected card being placed at the bottom of the pack without being exposed.

If the player decides to barter, he turns to the player on his left-hand side and offers a card, which must be exchanged for one of those in the next player's hand, unless that player considers his cards sufficiently strong to stand upon, in which case the winner is decided by the method just described.

If the player has traded, either for ready money or barter, and has secured a hand strong enough, he at once stands, and exposes his cards; if not, the dealer passes or to the next player, and acts in a similar manner, going round and round the table until one of the players decides to stand, when the hands are exposed and the round settled.

A player may only purchase or exchange one card at each turn; he must not do both, but he is compelled to do the one or the other, unless he decides to stand. When once a player agrees to stand, the commerce on that round ceases, and all the hands must be exposed. [74]

THE OLD GAME.

The older mode of playing the game of Commerce differs materially from the description given above, and as it does not present such chances, but is of a more limited character, it is not so interesting, nor does it afford so much scope for speculation and excitement.

The deal is decided and the cards are distributed in the same way as in the more modern game, but here an additional hand, of three cards, is dealt, and placed face upwards in the middle of the table. There is no trading with the dealer or any of the players, the operations of commerce being confined to the three cards exposed on the table. The player to the left of the dealer has the first turn, and he must either stand, pass, or exchange a card. In the latter case he takes one of those lying face upwards on the table, adds it to his hand, and places one of his own cards, face upwards, in place of the one removed. If the player passes, he says, "I pass," and is then debarred from afterwards exchanging any of his cards during that hand; while if he decides to stand, the next player decides what he will do, and so on round the table, until two of the players are satisfied with their hands, or all have declared to pass. If two of the players stand then each of the other players may make one more exchange (if they have not previously passed), and then the whole of the hands are exposed, just as described in connection with the modern game. There is no pool in this variation, the winner receiving instead the amount of the stake from each of the other players. In case of absolute equality between the two best hands, which may be regarded as an almost impossible event, then each of the winners receives a stake from all the other players. [75]

This is a variation of the old method of conducting the game, and is played on somewhat similar lines, except that a pool is made up, by each player paying in an equal sum, for which he receives three counters. Play then proceeds in the manner just described as the old game. The winner of the hand, instead of receiving a stake from each of the players, takes a previously arranged sum from the pool, while the player who has the worst hand puts one counter into the pool. The game continues until all but one of the players have exhausted their three counters, when the player who remains with the last counter or counters takes the amount left in the pool. As soon as a player has exhausted his counters he has to stand out of the game, and no cards are dealt to him, so that the adoption of this variation makes the game very tedious for those who are first out, as they may have to wait a considerable time before the stock of the other players is exhausted.

The player who is first out has the option of buying one counter from the pool, which is termed "buying a horse." He has to pay for the same into the pool such sum as may be agreed upon—usually one-third or one-half the amount of the original stake.

LIMITED COMMERCE.

It may be agreed that only the Tricon, Sequence, Flush, and Point shall be recognised in the game, or even Tricon, Sequence, and Point only; but the greater the number of combinations permissible the greater the enjoyment to be derived from the game, so that limitations of this character have little to recommend them. [76]

PENALTIES FOR THE DEALER.

It is sometimes agreed that when the dealer holds a Tricon, Sequence, Flush, or Pair, and his hand is beaten by either of the others, he has to pay the amount of a stake to each player, or only to those who have better hands than his. The former course will be found to be a severe tax on the dealer, and is not to be recommended. The dealer only has the same chances as the others, and such a penalty seems unjust.

EXTENDED COMMERCE.

This is only applicable to the modern mode of playing the game, which in this variation is extended until all the players are satisfied, that is, they may keep on trading, either for ready money or by barter, until they all receive cards sufficiently good to stand upon. The great objection to this variation is that it makes the game wearisome for those players who are soon enabled to stand, as they have to wait while the others are being satisfied.

CONTINUOUS DEALING.

Another method of playing the modern game is to allow the same dealer to remain in until one of the players secures a Tricon, Sequence, or Flush, when the deal passes to the next player, on the left-hand side. This variation is based on the same principle as governs the game of Vingt-un. [77]

SPECULATION.

This is a round game which for very many years has been one of the most popular of its class. It requires little skill in its conduct, being essentially a game of chance. The players do not look at their hands, and therefore cannot in any way influence their possibilities of success with the three cards dealt them. The only element of skill associated is in connection with the speculations which form part of the play, and which may be carried on by each of the players during its progress.

The ordinary packs of fifty-two or thirty-two cards may be used, and the number of players who may take part in the game is practically unlimited within the range of the pack; but it will be found that not more than ten players are desirable with the fifty-two card pack, and not more than six with the thirty-two card one, as otherwise too great a proportion of the pack is brought into use each deal, and there is not much scope for speculation as to what remains in the undealt portion of the pack.

In playing the game the ace is reckoned the highest card, then follow king, queen, knave, ten, *etc.*, down to two.

The first dealer is decided in the manner explained in connection with "Nap" (see page 9), and he has to pay two coins or counters into the pool, each of the other players contributing one. Three cards are then dealt to each player, one at a time, and going round from left to right. The top card remaining on the pack is turned up for trump, but [78] before turning it the dealer may sell it to any other of the players. If the dealer sells the turn-up card, the buyer becomes entitled to all the privileges that may ultimately attach to it, taking the entire amount in the pool if no higher trump is turned up during the progress of the hands.

The player next to the dealer, or if the dealer sold the turn-up card the one next to the purchaser, then turns up the top card of the three dealt him. If it proves to be a higher card of the trump suit than that already exposed, he becomes the chief hand, and may either retain the card, with the ultimate prospect of winning the pool, or he may sell it to either of the other players if a speculation can be arranged. If he sells the card, he passes it over to the purchaser, and the player on the left-hand side of the new holder becomes the next player. If the card turned up is not a trump, or is a lower trump than that already exposed, it is of no value, and the next player has to follow on with his top card.

The same proceeding is continued round and round until all the players, except the holder of the highest trump, have exposed their three cards. The owner of the leading trump, or the dealer, if he did not sell the turn-up and it remains unbeaten, does not expose his cards in the various rounds, but retains them until last. Even then he may sell them, before they are turned up, either singly or all together.

When all the cards have been exposed, the holder of the highest trump takes the amount in the pool, and a fresh deal, with new payments to the pool, is started upon.

If the card turned up proves to be an ace, king, queen, or knave, it is usual for the deal to pass. In that case the dealer, or the purchaser of the trump card if the dealer has sold it, takes the pool, when all the players contribute as before, the next in turn becoming the dealer, and using the next top card of the pack for his trump card. This method [79] saves the time of going all round with the hands, when with so high a card turned up there are so few chances of either of the players having a better one, as to virtually put an end to all speculation that hand.

During the progress of the game either of the players may sell the card which it is his turn to expose. In that case he turns it up without disturbing the order of play, and retains it if it is not a superior trump. If it is a superior one, it has to be handed over to the purchaser, and the player on his left has to proceed with the play.

The holder of the highest trump card may sell it at any time, so that it may change hands several times during the same deal, and each time there is a change the player on the buyer's left-hand side is the next to proceed.

Any player looking at a card out of turn has to pay a penalty into the pool, and should he prove the winner he cannot take the amount in the pool, but must leave it to be added to the stakes for the next deal.

It is sometimes agreed that the turn-up card shall belong to the pool, and in that case it is not offered for sale. If it proves the ultimate Winner of the round, the amount is left in the pool, and added to the stake for the next deal, the amount of which is made up just as if the previous one had been taken by one of the players.

A second method of benefiting the pool is to deal a spare hand, which is left in the middle of the table until all the other hands have been finished. The spare hand is then turned up, and if it contains a winning card the amount in the pool is added to the stake for the next round.

Another variation is to impose a penalty when a knave or five is turned up, the penalty being paid into the pool by the owner of the card, that is, the original holder or the purchaser if it was sold before being turned up. [80]

POPE JOAN.

For the game of Pope, or Pope Joan, a special board, or a pool with eight compartments, is required, or the divisions may be marked on a sheet of paper or card. The game is available for any number of players, and an ordinary pack of fifty-two cards is used, the eight of diamonds being taken out, so as to form what is termed a stop, that is, a break in the sequence of the cards, which are here reckoned in regular order from ace to king, the four suits being kept distinct throughout the play. The seven of diamonds thus becomes a stop, and the king of each Suit is also a stop, there being no "following" card in either case. The turn-up or trump card, as will be further explained later on, forms another stop, and thus there are six regular known stops at the commencement of each game, with a number of unknown ones caused by the cards in the spare hand which forms part of the game.

The object of the players is to dispose of their cards as rapidly as possible, under certain conditions, and the player who first succeeds in clearing his hand wins the stake set apart for game, as well as a contribution from the other players for each of the cards remaining in their hands. The holders of certain other cards secure the stakes contributed for them if they play them out during the progress of the hands. [81]

The earliest matter for consideration is to determine who shall be the first dealer, and that is settled in the same way as at "Nap" (see page 9). The players then contribute between them fifteen (or more) counters or coins to form a pool, the dealer giving double the amount paid by the other players. The counters or coins are then distributed so as to dress the eight divisions of the board, which are named as follows:— Pope Joan (the nine of diamonds), Matrimony (king and queen of trumps), Intrigue (queen and knave of trumps), Ace, King, Queen, Knave (of trumps), and Game, which latter is secured by the player who first succeeds in disposing of all the cards dealt him. Six of the counters are placed for Pope Joan, two each for Matrimony and Intrigue, one each for Ace, King, Queen, and Knave, and the remainder for Game. To save the trouble and time of collecting the stakes from the several players for each round, it is often agreed that the dealer for the time being shall dress the board, in which case it is necessary that the game should be finished just before the original dealer's turn comes round again, else the payments to the pool will not have been equitably divided.

The stakes being completed, the pack, from which the eight of diamonds has been removed, is shuffled and cut. The dealer then proceeds to distribute the cards, one at a time, as equally among the players as possible, dealing a spare hand, which is left unexposed on the table, for the purpose of forming further stops, and turning up the last card for trump. If any odd cards remain after dealing round to the players, it is best to add the surplus to the spare hand. For instance, with five players there will be eight cards for each hand, one to turn up, and two remaining; these two should be added to the spare hand. With eight players there will be five each, and five remaining; so [82] that the spare hand will be increased to ten, but that will only cause a greater number of stops, which will not prove any disadvantage with so many players engaged.

Should the trump card prove to be the nine of diamonds — Pope Joan, — the dealer takes the amount staked for that card, and, in addition, receives from each player a stake for every card dealt. If there are but few players engaged in the game, it is best to agree that the payment for Pope Joan shall be limited to either four or six counters or coins, and it may be best to do so, no matter what number of players are engaged. If the card turned up for trump be either Ace, King, Queen or Knave, the dealer takes whatever stake is deposited on the hoard in the corresponding division, and the game proceeds, as is also the case if any lower card is turned up.

During the progress of the game, the holder of Pope Joan, Matrimony, Intrigue, or Ace, King, Queen, or Knave of trumps can, if he has the opportunity, play those cards, in which event he takes the amount of the stake on the corresponding part of the board, and, in the case of Pope Joan, he receives a stake from every player for each card remaining in hand. Neither of these combinations or cards wins anything, however, if not played out during the progress of the game, and they can only be declared in the ordinary course of play. For this reason Pope Joan or ace of trumps should be led on the first opportunity, as neither of them can be played up to, each following a stop. When any or all of the special cards are not played out, the stake on their particular division of the board is left for the next deal, so that it may happen that either of the compartments except Game, which is won every deal, may be considerably increased before it is secured by one of the players. For this reason it is desirable to study the state [83] of the board, so as to see if the stake on any particular card in hand is sufficient to warrant its being played at an early stage, even though lower cards of the same suit are in hand, which would, in the ordinary course, be cleared off first.

It is sometimes agreed that when Intrigue or Matrimony is played by different hands, the amount staked on those chances shall be divided between the two-players concerned, and in each case the player of knave, queen, or king takes the stake on those chances in addition.

Play in the game is commenced by the elder hand, that is, the player on the left-hand side of the dealer, leading a card, to which the other players have to follow on in the same suit and in sequence, passing where they are unable to follow, until a stop occurs, when the competitor who plays the stop has the next lead. The played cards are turned over, face downwards on the table, after each stop. It must be remembered that the object of the players is to dispose of their cards as soon as possible, and on that account the known stops should be played out at the first opportunity, or led up to as early as possible.

To better explain the method of play, we will take an imaginary hand. We will suppose there are five players, and that the one on the dealer's left-hand side receives

5 and 7 of diamonds, 4 and knave of hearts,
knave and king of spades, ace and queen of clubs.

The turn-up card proves to be the 7 of hearts. The player thus knows he has two stops among his eight cards, *viz.*, the of diamonds and king of spades; but in each case he has lower cards of the same suit, and he must therefore consider how best to clear them off. The king of spades being a stop, and the player having the knave and king of that suit, [84] he cannot do wrong in leading the knave, as, if the queen is played he follows on with the king, and if by chance the queen should be in the spare hand, he still gets rid of the king, having to follow on, after his knave having proved a stop. The same argument holds good in the case of the diamonds, of which he first leads the five and clears the suit. The ace of clubs must next be played, as unless he leads that himself there is no possibility of his being able to play it, as no card can lead up to an ace. He therefore plays the club ace for his fifth card, the two and three follow on from different hands, and then a stop occurs, so that it is assumed the four is in the spare hand, and thus the three is a stop. The player of the three has, among his other cards, the queen and king of hearts, plays them (taking the stake on Matrimony, as hearts are trumps), and follows on with the seven of spades, of which he also holds the ten, which, as knave, queen, and king have been played, he knows to be a stop. By playing off queen and king of hearts, this player made the knave of hearts in the first hand a stop. Later on the game leads up to the queen of clubs, which also proves to be a stop, the king being in the spare hand, and the original leader is left with the lead with only two cards in hand, of which one is known to be a stop. He therefore first plays this knave of hearts, following on with his four, clearing his hand and winning the game. He takes the stake on Game from the board, and receives one counter from the other players for each card remaining in their hand, the only exception in such cases being in favour of the holder of Pope Joan, who is exempt if he has not played that card, but who has to pay as the rest if he has played it. [85]

VARIATIONS.

The most popular variation from the foregoing game is for the winner, *i.e.* the one who first plays out his cards, to only take the stake for Game from the board, the players paying to the pool the penalty for their unplayed card or cards, and distributing them on whichever chance they prefer, except that all the eight must be covered. In such a case the regular dressing of the board by the players at the commencement of each deal as previously described is omitted, the dealer alone paying a single stake, which he may also place where he chooses.

FIVE-POOL POPE.

The board or pool may be made with five divisions only, in which case Pope Joan, Matrimony, Intrigue, Ace, and Game are retained, King, Queen, and Knave being omitted. In other respects the game is conducted on the ordinary lines, except that twelve coins or counters are sufficient to dress the board.

POPE JOAN WINS.

In this variation, when Pope Joan is turned up the dealer at once wins the game, and takes the stake standing to Game on the board, in addition to that on Pope and the payment from each of the players already referred to. This is by no means a desirable innovation, and simply causes extra trouble for dealing, *etc.*, with little or no recompense.

LIMITED STOPS.

In lieu of the spare hand being dealt, with the object of making extra stops, it may be arranged that a definite [86] number of cards be taken from the pack, either from the top or the bottom, for the purpose, or the remainder, after dealing the cards round as far as possible equally among the players, may be so set apart. The best way, however, is to deal a spare hand with the others, as then the number of stops bears an equitable proportion to the number of players engaged in the game.

LOOKING AT THE SPARE HAND.

Among amateurs and inexperienced players it is sometimes agreed that the dealer shall look at the spare hand, so as to see what cards are stops; but after a few rounds have been played, the absurdity of this rule will be manifest. It gives so much advantage to the dealer, who can play cards which he alone knows to be stops,

that in such a case he ought to stand out, no cards being dealt him
that round. It is an altogether objectionable variation, and not at all
a necessary one.

Pope Joan is sometimes allowed to be played at any time in lieu
of a stop, thus: suppose a player has Pope and (say) knave of
spades. In the course of the game the nine of spades is played, and
proves to be a stop. The holder of Pope may play it in lieu of the ten
of spades, and then continue with his knave of that suit, first taking
his winnings on Pope. [87]

SPIN.

Spin may be regarded somewhat as a variation or offshoot of Pope Joan, which game it very much resembles. The dealer will therefore do well to refer to the description given of that game, on pages 81 to 87, for further and more extended details.

At Spin the two of hearts is taken out of the pack, in addition to the eight of diamonds, but in distributing the cards no spare hand is dealt, so that there are always six regular stops in the game. In addition, the ace of diamonds, which is called Spin, may also be used as a stop, if the player chooses to make it one, and he has the necessary card with which to follow, as explained later on.

There are only three pool chances to play for in this game: Matrimony (king and queen of diamonds), Intrigue (queen and knave of diamonds), and Game, or first out. In addition to these three chances, the holder of Spin receives a stake (usually three counters) from the other competitors, provided the card is played out in the ordinary course of the game; while each king entitles its holder to one counter from every competitor when they are played out. In both these cases the amounts must be collected before another card is played, or they are forfeited.

The pool is made by each player, except the dealer, paying in a stake for Game, while the dealer has to contribute a double stake to make a pool for Matrimony, and a single stake for Intrigue. He is sometimes called upon to con[88]tribute to Game also, but that is putting a tax upon him disproportionate to what is required from the other players.

The two of hearts and eight of diamonds having been taken out, the cards are shuffled and then dealt out, as near equally as possible, among the players. No turn-up card is needed, as there are no trumps in this game. The player on the dealer's left has the lead, and he proceeds in the manner described for Pope Joan (see page 84).

The holder of Matrimony or Intrigue can declare them at any time after he plays a stop, and he then takes the stake for those chances in the pool. He need not play the cards, but simply shows them, and may then follow on, as he has a right to do after a stop, with any card he chooses.

The holder of Spin can play it at any time when either of his other cards comes in sequence in the progress of the game, or after a stop. In the former case, the playing of Spin makes it a stop, but it must be played out with the card which follows on, or the holder loses his chance of playing it. For instance, suppose clubs are in play, that the six is the last card, and that the holder of the seven has Spin. He plays the two cards together, and says, "seven and Spin." The other competitors then pay him the agreed stake for Spin, and the game proceeds. If the holder of Spin does not succeed in playing it he has to pay double to the winner of the game for every card remaining in his hand.

When one of the players has played all his cards, he becomes the winner, and the others pay him a stake for each card remaining in their hands. In addition he takes the amount of the pool set apart for first out. The winner of the game is also exempt from payment towards the next pool for Game. If, however, the winner is the next dealer, then he has to contribute to Matrimony and Intrigue in the ordinary course. [89]

NEWMARKET.

This is another variation of Pope Joan, or Spin, and is played on similar lines. The seven of each suit is taken out to form stops, and four cards are turned up in the middle of the table. These must be the four principal cards, *viz.*, ace, king, queen, and knave, but of different suits, so that each of the four are represented in the pool; say, for example, knave of diamonds, queen of hearts, king of clubs, and ace of spades may be turned up.

The several players pay a coin or counter to form the first pool, and may put it on whichever card of the four turned up they choose, provided that all four are covered. The dealer pays one extra throughout the game. The whole of the cards are then dealt, as nearly equal as possible, as for Spin. Play proceeds as in that game, the holder of the card immediately preceding those in the pool taking the stake upon it when he plays his card. For this purpose the ace is considered both as lowest and highest, so that, in the supposed cases given above, the holders of king of spades, queen of clubs, knave of hearts, and ten of diamonds become winners of pool stakes on playing out their respective cards. These would in each case become stops, and the player would have the right to play another card.

The one who first succeeds in clearing his hand wins the game, and receives from each of the other competitors a stake for every remaining card. The pool stakes cannot be taken unless the cards are played up to, and if this is not done the amounts are carried on to the next deal. The hints and fuller explanation given in Pope Joan and Spin should be studied in connection with this game. [90]

SNIP-SNAP-SNORUM.

There are two distinct methods of playing this game, so unlike as to lead to the conclusion that at some time or other two separate games must have been confused by being called under the same name, and have since been so associated with each other. There is hardly one point in common between the two methods in vogue; and while one is entirely different from anything yet described in the present volume, the other is, to a great extent, played on the lines of Pope Joan, Spin, and Newmarket, and may be regarded as an offshoot of those games—rather than as an independent one—- which has got mixed with the one known under the title of Snip-Snap-Snorum, and has come to be recognised under that name. As preference in such a case should be given to the independent game, we shall first describe that, and afterwards devote attention to the other system. In doing so we must excuse ourselves for the manifest inconsistency of associating two distinct games under the one title, on the ground of custom and practice among different individuals, and in order to avoid confusion as far as possible, we have re-named the game we shall describe last, as Jig, that being one of the terms used in the game, and sufficiently distinctive for every purpose.

Snip-Snap-Snorum is a round game, available for any number, of players from two to ten, when the full pack of fifty-two cards is played with, or for any number up to six [91] when the smaller pack of thirty-two is used. Probably the best number of players is five or six in the former case, and three or four in the latter; the greatest objection to a large number of players being that those first out have to wait until the others have exhausted their stakes, which may not occur until several more rounds have been completed.

At the commencement of the game each player has to be provided with five coins or counters, of equal value, and the game is decided when all but one of the players has exhausted those five stakes. The player who holds out the longest becomes the winner, and secures the whole of the pool, which is contributed to during the progress of the game as described later on.

The deal is decided in the ordinary way, the player to whom the first knave is turned up having the first right to deal the cards. He shuffles the pack, has it cut, and then distributes five cards to each player, one at a time, and commencing with the one on his left-hand side. There is no turn-up card needed; when all have received their five cards the hands are looked at, and the game begins. The object of the players is to play cards of equal value to those of their right-hand adversaries, and if they do so the player has to pay a penalty into the pool; one stake for Snip, which is the first pairing of a card; two stakes for Snap, the second pairing of the same card; and three stakes for Snorum, the third pairing. For instance, suppose there are five players, *A, B, C, D,* and *E. A* is the dealer, and, the cards having been dealt, *B* has to lead; he plays a nine, and calls it when he places it on the table face upwards in front of him; *C* likewise has a nine, which he must play by also placing it face upwards on the table in front of him, and says "Snip," upon which *B* has to pay a stake into the pool, his card having been paired *D* also has [92] a nine, which he plays in similar manner, and says "Snap," upon which *C* has to pay two stakes into the pool, his card having been also paired; *E* then has to follow on, and also having a nine in hand, he must play it, and says "Snorum," which imposes a penalty of three stakes upon *D*. This having disposed of the four nines in the pack, *A*, whose turn it now is to play, has to start upon a new card, and he has the option of playing whichever of the five in his hand he chooses.

The penalties of Snip-Snap-Snorum do not remain in force if any other card intervenes between the pairs, so that it is only the player next in order of play who has the opportunity of securing a stack& for the pool from any of the others. Taking the illustration given above, we will suppose that *D* had no nine, and was accordingly compelled to play, say, a ten. *B* would have had to pay the penalty for Snip, as before; but *C* could have nothing to pay, his card not having been paired. Then suppose *E*, in his turn, played a nine, and *A* also played one, that would only "snip" *E's* nine, although the other two nines had just been played; *E* would have to pay one stake to the pool.

As soon as the five cards dealt to each player are exhausted, the next in order becomes the dealer, and distributes five cards to each player, as before, and the game is conducted round and round on exactly similar lines until one of the party has lost the last of his five stakes. He is then out of the game, and if he has any cards left he must add them, face downwards and unexposed, to the top of the undealt portion of the pack. The other players proceed with the game, and as each loses his last stake he is left out, and no fresh cards are dealt him. This goes on until all but one have lost their stakes, when, as already described, the game is finished, and the last in takes the pool. [93]

If a new game is started on, the first out in the previous game becomes the new dealer.

The lead is a disadvantage in this game, as, after a few cards have been played, it is often possible to know that certain cards remaining in hand are absolutely safe, or nearly so. For instance, suppose two knaves have been played during the first round or two, and that a third knave is in a player's hand, that card may be played as an almost safe one, as there is only one other that can pair with it, and the odds of the fourth knave being in the next player's hand are very remote. For the same reason a player having two of a kind in his own hand should always play one of them when his turn comes round, provided, of course, he is not able to pair with the player immediately preceding him.

If a player has a card similar to that played immediately before him, he must play it. In the event of his failing to do so, he has to pay a double penalty to the pool, while the player who would have been penalized has to contribute just as though the right card had been played. These penalties must be enforced before the cards are cut for the next deal.

VARIATIONS.

This method of playing the game is sometimes varied as follows: Instead of dealing five cards to each player, the whole of the pack is distributed, equally, or as nearly equal as possible, among the players, each of whom starts with five coins or counters, as in the other game. The player on the dealer's left-hand side, whom we will call *B*, as above, has to lead, and he keeps on playing one card after another until the opponent on his left (*C*) can pair one of them. When *C* succeeds in doing this, he says "Snip," and *B* has to pay a stake into the pool, while he remains in [94] active until the game has proceeded right round the table. Play now rests between *C* and *D*. If *D* can pair *C's* card with which he snipped *B* he does so, and calls "Snap," when *C* has to pay two stakes to the pool; if then *E* can also pair the card, he cries "Snorum," and *D* has to pay three stakes to the pool. If, however, the players cannot pair, then *C* has to keep on playing out his cards until *D* can pair one, in which case *C* is snipped, and the game proceeds as just described. The game goes round until all have played their cards, when the pack is again shuffled, and a new deal started upon, the game being won and the stakes secured by the player who holds out the longest with his five stakes, as in the other game.

This variation may be altered again by agreeing that an unlimited number of coins or counters may be used, and that the player who first succeeds in getting rid of his cards shall be the winner of the pool. By this system each deal becomes complete in itself, but it will not be found a very desirable innovation if many players are engaged, as in that case the cards are so divided that it becomes an easy matter to clear a hand.

TURN-UP SNIP.

It is sometimes agreed that the dealer shall turn up the top card of the undealt portion of the pack, and if then the first player can match it, the dealer has to pay the penalty for Snip. A much better way of playing this variation, however, is for the pool to pay the penalty for this first Snip. In that case the player takes one counter out of the pool and adds it to his own stock. [95]

JIG.

We have already mentioned that our reason for adopting the above title is to distinguish this method of playing the game of Snip-Snap-Snorum from the one just described, and it will be evident to those who study the two systems that we are quite justified in introducing a distinctive name for the one we are now about to deal with, which, as we have said, has little or nothing — beyond former title and use of similar terms — in common with the other.

The first dealer having been settled, and the pack shuffled, the cards are dealt out one at a time until the pack is exhausted. The object of the players is to get rid of their cards as speedily as possible, the one first out winning a coin or counter from each of the other players for every card remaining in their hands. The player on the dealer's left-hand side has to play first, and he leads whichever card he chooses, placing it face upwards on the table in front of him, and saying "Snip"; the holder of the next highest card of the same suit (ace counting as lowest and king as highest) has to follow on, and says "Snap"; then the three next highest cards are played, the holders of them saying "Snorum," "Hicockalorum" and "Jig" respectively, when playing them. The one who plays Jig has the next lead, and may follow on with whichever card he chooses. If either of the cards played is a stop, — that is to say, the succeeding card has been played out, or it is a king, — then the player says "Jig" after announcing what card he plays, as, for [96] instance, "Snip-Jig," "Snap-Jig," and so on. The player of the stop has to lead the next card.

It will thus be seen that the object of the players should be to lead such cards as will bring the Jig into their own hand again whenever possible, as then another card has to be led, and a greater chance exists of clearing the hand. To do this successfully, it is necessary to remember what cards are played during the progress of the game, so as to know which are stops, and then, if the stops are in hand, such cards should be played as would lead up to them. It will be well to bear in mind the following, which gives a list of the "Jigs" to the several cards of the pack: —

The five is	"Jig" to	the ace.	The ten is	"Jig" to	six.
" six	"	two.	" knave	"	seven.
" seven	"	three.	" queen	"	eight.
" eight	"	four.	" king	"	nine, ten,
" nine	"	five.		knave or	queen.

Similarly, if the two, three, or four is a stop, the ace, two or three may be played so as to lead up to them and thus secure the Jig.

When one of the party has exhausted his cards, he says "Out," and then receives a coin or counter from each player for every card they have left, and he also wins the amount in the pool if one has been formed. This is possible in many ways: either by each player contributing to it equally, by calling upon the dealer to pay in, or by the infliction of fines or penalties for incorrect calls, *etc.*

It is hardly necessary to give further details of the method of playing the hands, the game being so similar to Pope Joan, Spin, and Newmarket, which are fully described elsewhere. Players will do well to refer to those games for further information in regard to this variation of Snip-Snap-Snorum. [97]

CASSINO.

———

This game, which is of considerable antiquity, is available for two, three, four, or more persons, but is usually played by four, when two of the players act as partners against the other two. It is, however, equally available for four players acting independently, in which case each scores his individual points, whereas in the partnership game, as with only two players, the lesser number of points is taken from the greater, and the difference only is scored by the winner. With three players it is also necessary to score independently, although in all these independent scorings it is sometimes decided that the lowest scorer shall not reckon anything, while the number of his points is deducted from those of each of the others; as, for instance: suppose A made 1 point, B 2, C 3 and D 5; A would not score anything, while B would score 1, C 2, and D 4. Similarly, if A made 2 points, B 2, C 2 and D 5; D would be the only one to score, and he would count 3.

It is usual to play with the full pack of fifty-two cards; there is however no reason why the smaller pack of thirty-two should not be used, but in that case the hands would be of shorter duration.

Assuming that four persons intend to take part in the game, and that they decide to play in pairs, the first question to settle will be as to who shall be partners, and who the first dealer. This is arranged by each of the four [98] players taking a card from the top or other part of the pack, when those who draw the two lowest cards have to play against the drawers of the two highest. The lowest of the four (ace counting as lowest) becomes the first dealer. In the event of a tie, which prevents the decision being thus made, only those whose cards are alike draw a second time. The partners sit opposite to each other, and the cards of each player are kept distinct until the hands are completed by the entire pack having been played through.

The cards having been shuffled and cut, the dealer distributes four cards to each of the players, dealing them one at a time. He also places four other cards face upwards in the middle of the table. It is usual to deal these latter one at a time when going round with the regular hands, but they may be taken all at one time from the top of the pack, after the players have received their cards. The player on the left-hand side of the dealer then plays a card from his own hand, and takes with it every card of the same denomination among those exposed on the table, as well as all that will combine and make the same number. For instance, a ten not only takes every other ten, but also nine and ace, eight and two, seven and three, six and four, or two fives, two threes and a four, and other combinations.

If the player is able to pair or combine any of the cards, he places them with his own card face downwards on the table in front of him; but if he is not able to pair or combine, he must add a card, face upwards, to those already exposed on the table. The next player does the same, and so on round the table until the four cards in hand have either been paired, combined, or added to the exposed stock on the table. The original dealer then distributes four fresh cards to each of the players, but does not expose any on the table as in the first round. The same proceeding [99] is repeated until the whole pack has been exhausted, the player who is last able to pair or combine any of the exposed cards taking all the remaining cards off the table, and scoring one point for thus "sweeping the board," as it is termed. If a player is able to sweep the board at any other time during the progress of the game, he also scores a point, and the following player has to commence a new board by laying out a card.

The whole of the cards having thus been played, the partners combine their winnings, and the counting of the cards commences, the various points of the game being as follow:

The winner of Great Cassino (the ten of diamonds) reckons ... ...   2 points.

The winner of Little Cassino (the two of spades) reckons ... ...   1 point.

The winner of each ace reckons ... ...   1 "

The winner of the majority of the cards of the spade suit reckons ... ...   1 "

The winner of the majority of the entire pack of cards   3 points.

reckons ... ...

The partners whose winnings show the greater number of points then deduct the points of their opponents from their own, and score the remainder to their game; thus, if one sides secures 6, and the other side 5, the former score 1 point and the latter score nothing; while if the respective scores were 7 and 4, the winners of the seven points would add to their score.

The object of those engaged in the game being to secure Great Cassino, Little Cassino, the four aces, the majority of spades, and the greater number of cards, a few rules will at once suggest themselves to guide the play of the hands. [100] Secure the Cassino cards on the first opportunity, also aces and spades, after which aim to make as many combinations as possible, leaving the pairs until last, unless they be the ten or the two, which are always best got off the board as early as possible, so as to prevent the opponents making the Cassinos if they have them in hand.

When three players are engaged, it is sometimes agreed that the two lowest shall add their points together, and subtract them from the highest. In such a case, if the two lower numbers together either amount to or exceed the higher, then neither party scores. This method will not be found desirable in actual play, as it leads to so many hands resulting in a negative score.

If a card is exposed by the dealer in the first round, other than those dealt for the exposed hand, then the deal is forfeited, but the exposure of a card at a subsequent period does not disqualify the dealer, the player being compelled to take the exposed card, although it is best to impose some penalty for the fault. [101]

MY BIRD SINGS.

This game may be played by any number of persons up to thirteen, if a full pack of cards be used; or by any number up to eight with the smaller pack of thirty-two cards. A pool is formed by each player contributing a counter or coin, the dealer paying one extra. Four cards are then dealt to each player, and all have the right to look at their hands.

The object of the players is to secure a flush, four cards of one suit; or four cards of different suits; and when either of these combinations is secured, the player says: "My Bird sings," and he becomes the winner, and thereby entitled to the amount in the pool.

There are two methods of conducting the game: either by each player in turn throwing out a card from his hand, or by allowing the opponent on his left-hand side to take one.

The competitor on the dealer's left is the first to play, and, supposing his "Bird" does not already "sing," and the first-named method is adopted, he throws out one of his cards, face downwards, on the table. The player on his left adds this card to his own four, and if his "Bird" does not "sing," he in like manner throws one of his cards out for the next player; the same plan being adopted round and round, until one of the players secures the four cards necessary.

If the second method is adopted the player does not [102] himself reject a card, but turns his hand, without exposing it, to the next player, who selects whichever card he chooses, and proceeds with the game as in the other variation.

After going completely round among the players three times, the original leader may exchange one of his cards for the top card of the undealt portion of the pack, and if it should happen to be of the same suit as the one he threw out, he rejects it, and takes the next or following one, until he gets a different suit; but before introducing a new card into the game he must throw out one of those in hand. This introduction of new cards may be made each round, after the first three of a hand, until one of the players secures a winning set of cards, otherwise it may be a tedious matter to get a winning combination.

VARIATIONS.

The game is sometimes played for flushes only; that is, the four cards must be of one suit before a player's "Bird sings," and sometimes only three cards are dealt to each player, in which latter case flushes alone are recognised.

The game may also be continued until the whole pack of cards is exhausted; in which case, whenever a player's bird sings, he turns the four cards over and regards them as one trick. Four other cards are then given him from the top of the undealt portion of the pack, and the game proceeds as before. The ultimate winner is he who secures the greatest number of tricks. In the case of a tie the stakes are divided between the two or more players who have an equal number. [103]

96

SPOIL-FIVE

———

Spoil-Five may be played by any number of persons not exceeding ten; the best game, however, is when four or live take part, as then about half the cards are in play. In this game the cards run in different order to the ordinary course, vary in the two colours, and further, change in the trump suit, as follows:

1. *In Hearts and Diamonds, when not trumps.* — King, queen, knave, 10, 9, down to ace (the ace of hearts is always a trump card, and never counts as a heart).

2. *In Clubs and Spades, when not trumps.* — King, queen, knave, ace, 2, down to 10.

3. *In Hearts and Diamonds, when trumps.* — 5, knave, ace of hearts, ace of trumps, king, queen, 10, 9, 8, 7, 6, 4, 3, 2. (If hearts are trumps, there is only one ace.)

4. *In Clubs and Spades, when trumps.* — 5, knave, ace of hearts, ace of trumps, king, queen, 2, 3, 4, 6, 7, 8, 9, 10.

A simple method of remembering the order of the cards is to notice that the highest of the minor ones are the best in the red suits, and the lowest in the black ones.

A pool is made up by each player contributing two or three coins or counters for the purpose, the dealer paying an additional stake. The pool thus formed goes to the player who succeeds in winning three tricks in one hand; but if neither player succeeds in doing so, the game is said to be "spoilt," and the amount remains in the pool, the players contributing for the next round only one coin or [104] counter, and paying that number into the pool each deal until one of the party succeeds in winning three tricks, when he takes the total amount in the pool, and a new one is started by each player contributing the full stake as at the commencement. The dealer pays the sum agreed for the deal each time, no matter whether the pool was won, or the game spoilt, the previous round.

If there are only two players engaged, or with four, if it is agreed that two of the players combine against the other two, there can be no spoils, as one must win three of the tricks, and thus secure the pool, each round.

To determine the first dealer, the cards are dealt round as in "Nap" (see p. 9), when the player to whom the first knave falls becomes dealer. He shuffles the pack, has it cut by the player on his right-hand side, and proceeds to distribute five cards to each player, dealing them in regular order from left to right, and either first two and then three to each player, or first three and then two. The top card of the undealt portion of the pack is turned up for trump, and if it proves to be the ace, the dealer has the option of "robbing," as explained hereafter; and if it is not the ace, any one holding that card must rob before he plays, before his turn comes round.

If the dealer makes a misdeal, or deals out of order, or exposes a card, he loses his turn of dealing, and the next player in order takes his place; or it may be agreed that in case of a misdeal the dealer shall have the option of dealing again after paying a second stake for dealing into the pool. The deal is an advantage, and in case of a slip in the distribution of the cards, it will generally be found best to pay the penalty and deal again.

The game is opened by the player on the left-hand side of the dealer leading whichever of his cards he chooses. [105] If the card led be a trump, then all the players must follow suit if they are able to do so, subject to certain exceptions explained below under the heading of "Reneging."

If the ace of hearts is led, and another suit is trumps, it does not necessitate all the players following suit, even though the ace of hearts is always reckoned as a trump. The lead in this case is considered as made from a plain suit, and the rules governing them are enforced.

If the card is not a trump, then the other players may trump the card, or follow suit, as they please, but each must do the one or the other if he holds a card of the suit led if he does not hold one of the suit, then he may discard either of the others, or play a trump, as he prefers. The player of the highest card of the suit led, or of the highest trump, if trumps have been played, wins the trick, and he plays first to the next. In deciding the winner the cards are reckoned in the special order given above.

The game is continued until one player wins three tricks, when he takes the pool; or, failing that, till all of the cards are played, when the game is spoilt, and each contributes to the pool the reduced stake agreed upon.

ROBBING.

Robbing is one of the most important features of the game, inasmuch as if the player who holds the ace of trumps omits to rob when his turn comes round, he is de-barred from winning the pool that hand, even though he may secure the necessary number of tricks.

The method of robbing if the ace is turned up, is for the dealer to place one of his own cards on the table face downwards in front of him, which card must not be exposed at any time during the progress of the hand. He does not take the ace into his own hand until the others [106] have played to the first trick, but when it comes to his turn he adds it to his hand, or he may at once use it. He must, however, throw out the card with which he intends to rob the ace before the first card of the round is played, and reasonable time must be allowed to do so. The turn-up suit remains trump throughout the hand.

In the case of the ace not being turned up, and being in the hand of either of the players, then the holder must rob the turn-up card when it comes to his turn to play to the first trick. The manner of doing this is somewhat similar to that just described; the holder of the ace rejects a card placing it face downwards on the table, and takes the turn-up card into his hand. He must do this when it is his turn to play, and before showing his first card, otherwise he forfeits the privilege, and is, moreover, prohibited from winning the pool that round, no matter how many tricks he may secure. The same penalty is attached to the player who robs the turn-up card without holding the ace.

As a variation, it may be agreed that robbing shall be optional, or shall not be recognised as a part of the game.

RENEGING.

The holder of the five of trumps, the knave of trumps, or the ace of hearts, enjoys the privilege of not being obliged to play them when a trump is led; but this privilege (which is called reneging) only holds when the trump led is a lower one. For instance, if the knave be led, the holder of the ace of hearts is obliged to play it.

VARIATIONS.

A very good game may be played by allowing the cards to retain their ordinary sequence. As this avoids confusion, it is more suitable for family play. [107]

TWO TRICKS WIN.

If five or more players are taking part in the game, it may be found desirable that the winner of two tricks shall take the pool, or partnerships can be formed; otherwise a long continuation of spoils may occur.

FIVING.

This variation is sometimes played when two persons, or two sets of partners are engaged in the game. It consists in allowing the non-dealer, providing he is not satisfied with his cards, to ask the dealer to "five" it, when, if the dealer agrees, the trump card is removed, and the next card is turned up for trump. If that proves to be of the same suit as the original turn-up, the next is taken, and so on until a change occurs. The right to five can only be exercised once each hand.

JINKING.

A variation is sometimes made by the introduction of "jinking." The winner of all five tricks receives from each player his original stake in addition to the amount in the pool; if, however, any player who has won three tricks goes on playing, thinking he can jink, and fails to do so, he loses the pool which he would otherwise have won for his three tricks.

TWENTY-FIVE AND FORTY-FIVE.

Instead of the game being finished in one hand, it may continue until one player makes twenty-five, or forty-five. In this case there are no spoils, and every trick scores five to the winner. Any player "jinking," *i.e.*, winning the five tricks, wins the game. [108]

LOTO.

———

There are many varieties of Loto, with pictures, flowers, letters, *etc.*, instead of numbers, which are known as Picture Loto, Botanical Loto, Spelling Loto, Geographical Loto, Historical Loto, and so on.

These are mostly games for children, and are played in exactly the same way as numbered Loto.

This game in England is usually regarded as an amusement for young children; but it is one capable of affording amusement to grown-up people, as may be seen by the interest shown in "Keno" by the Americans.

"Keno," or American Loto, is played in various places of public resort, by adults, for considerable stakes, and is esteemed capital practice in reading numbers rapidly and correctly.

The requisite paraphernalia for this game—which may be played by any number of persons, not exceeding twenty-four—are boxes containing 100 counters; 14 fishes, each of which is reckoned as 10 counters; 12 contracts, valued at 10 fish or 100 counters apiece; a pack of 24 very large cards with fifteen different numbers marked on each, and a bag containing 90 knobs or discs, numbered from 1

5	11		33		50		76	
	17	22		43		65		89
2		28	35		56		74	

Fig. 1.

to 90.

In addition, a board with ten cavities cut therein for the purpose of placing the knobs as drawn, is required. [109]

A Loto card, on which are inscribed, in the manner shown in the diagram, numbers ranging from 1 to 90 — five numbers on each line, is represented in fig 1. The units are arranged in the first column, the tens in the second, the twenties in the third, and so on.

The number of these cards supplied in a Loto box varies, but the general number is twenty-four, although sometimes there are only eighteen. With twenty-four cards, each number appears in four different cards.

There are several different methods of playing this game, of which we will give the two principal ones. The first method makes it a game of chance and skill, or rather quickness in reading figures; and the second, purely a game of luck.

First Method. — Before commencing the game, a dealer has to be chosen, and his duties consist of shuffling the cards and dealing to each player one or more cards. The dealer is unable to join in the game, and is obliged to stand out.

Each player should stake a certain sum, which should be reserved for the winner; and a certain number of counters of no value, but merely to be used for covering the numbers as called, should be placed in the pool.

Sometimes each player contributes a certain number of counters to the pool, then each saves out of his stake the number of counters he has on his card or cards; and the winner obtains the money for his fifteen counters on his card, and receives in addition all the pool which remains.

In order to render the game still more interesting, the contributions to the pool should be so arranged that it is capable of being divided into four parts. Then a fourth part of the pool is won by the player who first succeeds in covering one horizontal row; another fourth part of the [110] pool is won by the player who first succeeds in covering two horizontal rows, and the remaining half is reserved for the winner who first covers the whole of his card.

The dealer then, having deposited the 90 knobs in a bag, draws them forth rapidly, one by one, and calls out the number which appears or the knob in a clear tone.

The player, having the corresponding number on his cards or cards, who first answers to the number called, covers the number on the card or cards with one of the counters in the pool, which should be so placed on the table as to be available for the use of all the players.

The player who first succeeds in covering all the numbers on his card or cards wins the game.

The Second Method.—Every player should draw two cards, and deposit a stake previously agreed upon; and if the party is not too numerous, then any may take four or six cards, laying down a double or treble stake accordingly; and when the players are more than twelve, then some are only to have one card, paying half a stake, and likewise should the players not take all the cards among them, the remainder of the pack is to be laid aside until some other persons join the set. From the cards not taken, players may exchange one or more of those drawn, or they may change with one another; similar exchanges, if the company consent, may also be made previous to each drawing, and likewise prior to replenishing the pool. Cards may be thrown up, or additional ones drawn from those put by; stakes being paid proportionably.

The stakes are to be put together in a pool, placed in the middle of the table, and also on the table there should be a quantity of counters sufficient for the number of cards taken; upon the counters a value is to be fixed adequate to the stakes first deposited, from the whole of which a sum [111] must be reserved, enough to pay, at the conclusion of the game, all the counters laid upon the table.

Then, after counting the 90 knobs, so as to be certain they are right, the eldest hand shall first shake them well together in the bag, and afterwards draw out ten successively, not only declaring the number of each as drawn, but also placing the same conspicuously on the board.

As soon as a number is declared, each player having that number on one or more of his cards, is to take up counters, sufficient to lay one upon that number every time it occurs, and so on until the ten knobs are drawn. When only part of the pack is taken, and a number drawn happens not to be upon any player's card, then the players may put away that knob till some person takes a card on which it is printed.

When ten knobs are drawn out, every player examining the cards separately, and having only one counter upon any horizontal line, wins for that no more than the said counter, which is styled gaining by *abstract;* where two counters are on the same horizontal line of a separate card, the player gains an *ambo,* and becomes entitled to five counters besides the two; when three are upon the same line, the player obtains a *terne,* and is to receive 25 additional counters; if four are on the same line, that is called a *quaterne* winning 100 counters additional; when five occur on the same line, that makes a *quinterne,* gaining 250 additional counters, and the player is entitled to payment out of the pool for all the above-mentioned acquisitions previous to another drawing. Instead of giving counters, payment for the same may at once be made from the stock in the pool.

The knobs are then to be returned, and the bag given to the next player in rotation, who is to shake the same, and draw, *etc.,* as before stated. [112]

Whenever the pool is exhausted, the players must contribute again, according to the number of cards taken; and when it is resolved to finish the game, they agree among themselves to have only a fixed number of drawings more.

At the last drawing each player proceeds as heretofore directed, but the drawing concludes when no more counters are left on the table. The players then, beginning with the eldest hand, are to be paid out of the pool, as far as the money will go; and when that is expended, the others remain unpaid, which is styled a Bankruptcy; lastly, the players should re-unite the counters obtained from the pool with those that were on their cards, and receive payment for them out of the fund reserved at the commencement of the game.

The counters requisite for the payment of the players are:—

For	24	Cards	144		Times Ten.
"	18	"	108		"
"	12	"		72	"
"	6	"		36	"

Consequently, 60 counters should be contributed for every card taken by a player.